The Teaching for Social Justice Series

William Ayers
Series Editor

Therese Quinn
Associate Series Editor

Editorial Board: Hal Adams, Barbara Bowman, Lisa Delpit, Michelle Fine,
Maxine Greene, Caroline Heller, Annette Henry, Asa Hilliard, Rashid Khalidi,
Gloria Ladson-Billings, Charles Payne, Mark Perry, Luis Rodriguez,
Jonathan Silin, William Watkins

Teaching Science for Social Justice
ANGELA CALABRESE BARTON, with JASON L. ERMER,
TANAHIA A. BURKETT, and MARGERY D. OSBORNE

Putting the Children First:
The Changing Face of Newark's Public Schools
JONATHAN G. SILIN and CAROL LIPPMAN, Editors

Refusing Racism:
White Allies and the Struggle for Civil Rights
CYNTHIA STOKES BROWN

A School of Our Own:
Parents, Power, and Community at the East Harlem Block Schools
TOM RODERICK

The White Architects of Black Education:
Ideology and Power in America, 1865–1954
WILLIAM WATKINS

The Public Assault on America's Children:
Poverty, Violence, and Juvenile Injustice
VALERIE POLAKOW, Editor

Construction Sites:
Excavating Race, Class, and Gender Among Urban Youths
LOIS WEIS and MICHELLE FINE, Editors

Walking the Color Line:
The Art and Practice of Anti-Racist Teaching
MARK PERRY

A Simple Justice:
The Challenge of Small Schools
WILLIAM AYERS, MICHAEL KLONSKY, and
GABRIELLE H. LYON, Editors

Holler If You Hear Me:
The Education of a Teacher and His Students
GREGORY MICHIE

Teaching Science for Social Justice

Angela Calabrese Barton

with Jason L. Ermer, Tanahia A. Burkett, and Margery D. Osborne

TEACHERS
COLLEGE
PRESS

Published by Teachers College Press, 1234 Amsterdam Avenue, New York, NY 10027

Library of Congress Cataloging-in-Publication Data

Barton, Angela Calabrese.
    Teaching science for social justice / Angela Calabrese Barton, with Jason L. Ermer, Tanahia A. Burkett & Margery D. Osborne.
      p.   cm.—(The teaching for social justice series)
    Includes bibliographical references and index.
    ISBN 0-8077-4384-4 (cloth : alk. paper)—ISBN 0-8077-4383-6 (pbk. : alk. paper)
      1. Science—Study and teaching—Social aspects—United States—Case studies.
2. Science—Study and teaching (Elementary)—Activity programs—United States—Case studies.   3. Poor children—Education—Social aspects—United States—Case studies.
4. Education, Urban—Social aspects—United States—Case studies.   5. Social justice—United States—Case studies. I. Title. II. Series.

LB1585.3.B37 2003
372.3'5044—dc21   2003048445

ISBN 0-8077-4383-6 (paper)
ISBN 0-8077-4384-4 (cloth)

Printed on acid-free paper
Manufactured in the United States of America

10 09 08 07 06 05 04 03   8 7 6 5 4 3 2 1

Contents

Contents

excited voices. These children ranged in age from 5 to 11. We knew all the children well, as each of them had been deeply involved in Science Club. As we were walking over to see what had caught the children's attention, one of the older children, Juan,[1] witnessed our approach and quickly instructed the other children, "Get up! Angie's coming!" Three of the children stood up quickly, while one remained close to the ground, abruptly placing several old, broken pieces of particle board in a small space between the bottom of the fence and the ground. This space appeared to be wider and deeper than any of the other areas along the fence. Another child excitedly pointed to the space, saying that she thought an animal had tried to dig a tunnel under the fence and that they were trying to repair it with the wood before some of the younger children got hurt.

The fence (and the tunnel underneath it) that was the center of the children's attention that day was located near the back of Hope and served as the main boundary separating the housing units, where the children and their families lived, from the portable and playground (see Figure 1.1). The fence itself was large and imposing, nearly 10 feet tall, and made of long, black metal stakes spaced about 5 inches apart. There was one gate in the fence that allowed children and adults passage between the common housing area and the play area around the portable. However, the gate was only unlocked during the after-school hours while after-school activities operated for the children. It remained locked at all other times: in the morning,

Figure 1.1. Black security fence at Hope Shelter.

during the school day, in the evening, and on the weekends. During our tenure in the after-school programs at this shelter, many of the children, frustrated by their limited access to the only playground near their homes, requested that the gate remain open in the evenings and on weekends.

Although curious about the children's activity near the fence that day and of their desire to "block the animal hole so that other children did not get hurt," we chose, for the time being, to respect their secrecy and not to pursue their activities. After our brief exchange around the tunnel, all five children willingly left it alone, without any further explanation, to participate in Science Club (we were tending caterpillars and preparing seedlings for a butterfly garden). The next week, however, we found the children by the same tunnel again; only this time, the space under the fence was larger and deeper. Once the children saw us approaching them again, the youngest child of the group, 5-year-old Marc, ran up to us with his arms in the air and exclaimed how they had finally dug a tunnel under the fence deep enough for him to crawl through. He declared that he and the other small children could now gain access to the playground at night and on weekends, when the gate was locked. Marc's pronouncement was greeted with fierce responses from the other children, particularly the older children, who realized their secret was out. When the children realized that we were not angry at them, they shared with us that their plans were to continue to dig the tunnel deep enough for the older children to get through.

In many ways it was not surprising that the children dug such a tunnel. Their play spaces were severely limited. After 6 P.M. on school days and for much of the weekend, when there were no social workers present, students could not play on the playground or with the toys and games that were available in the Children's Activities Portable. The apartments surrounded a large, open courtyard where the students could play; however, the children preferred the playground, which had swings, a slide, and a number of climbing structures, all of which stood in the middle of a large sandbox, and the fact that the playground was not always available to them had been disappointing and frustrating to many of the students.

Fences have been commonplace at the shelters where we have worked. In fact, the entirety of Hope Shelter was surrounded by large, black security fences, which in certain sections were topped with barbed wire. Additional interior fences surrounded the housing facilities and separated them from other activity spaces, such as the Children's Activity Portable, the resource building, and the parking lot. When entering the shelter, drivers of vehicles had to pass through two sets of motorized access gates, waiting for the first gate to close behind them before the second gate would open. Security cards controlled the motorized access gates at the entry to the supportive housing parking lot as well as the gates that led to the apartₘₑₙₜ buildings. Residents, employees, volunteers, and guests were required to sign in and out, and while on the premises, all nonresidents were required to wear identification badges.

Given all these security measures, it was not surprising that the children of Hope, like the children and youth at other shelters where we have worked, continually referred to their surroundings as like a prison. At the same time, however, many of the children showed a particularly complex emotional response to their physical surroundings, recognizing the benefit of the security in ensuring their safety. Maria, a 9-year-old fourth grader who had been living at Hope for about a year when we met her, expressed this tension when describing things she thought should be changed about Hope:

> Don't leave us all crowded in. I mean like there are apartments and then there's a fence around the whole thing, and then there's another extra one. We're not, we're not in jail or nothing. And this looks like we're in jail. But it feels better because last time these three men had a gun and weed and they were by the trash can and my brother and his friends had to go throw away the trash. And they had to rollerblade fast because they were shooting a gun up. It's better with a fence but it looks too crowded. At least take the one down in here.

Maria's conflicting feelings of security and imprisonment have been echoed by other students, as have her observations about drug and gun use in the surrounding neighborhood.

Why do we begin this book with a story about the children digging a tunnel underneath a fence—a story that in many ways does not seem to have much to do with science or science education? After all, children dig holes in the earth all the time, for many different reasons, and most of the time their reasons are not very scientific. They are just digging to dig, not to explore the composition of soil or to design the best features for the most effective shovel or tunnel.

Yet we believe that this story about the children's decision to dig such a tunnel speaks volumes about their lives and how children constructively respond to the circumstances that frame those lives. We witnessed how the children devised this group activity to solve their problem of needing a place to play. We were impressed that they kept it a secret for so long (we learned about the purpose of the hole before the social workers at the supportive housing complex did) and that the children were able to use old, trashed pieces of particle board and kitchen spoons to dig a hole deep enough in the Texas earth (largely composed of hard topsoil and rock) for them to crawl through. Indeed, we have chosen to open this book with the tunnel story because it raises a series of questions about how children, and in this case, urban children in poverty, come to construct themselves and the kinds of things they do in relation to their social, cultural, political, and economic environments:

- What concerns do young people living in urban poverty have? How do they understand, articulate, and respond to these concerns? How do these concerns frame their lives?
- How do high-poverty, urban youth construct a practice of science in their lives in ways that are enriching, empowering, and transformative? In what ways does their practice of science intersect with the issues that frame their lives?
- How might the science teaching practice we construct formally (in school and out of school) with young people in urban poverty reflect their lives, their concerns, and their practices of science?

These questions—questions that emerge from the lives of urban youth struggling for authorship of their lives and of the science in their lives—are the questions that guide this book.

This book is the culmination of 6 years of teaching and researching science education from a critical/feminist perspective with urban youth in two different urban geographic locations (central Texas and New York City). The purpose of this book is to tell the stories of the lives of the youth with whom we have worked. In telling their stories, we hope to illustrate how their unique positions, as youth growing and learning in high-poverty, urban settings, frame their constructions of science in particularly compelling and challenging ways. On the one hand, the youth's lives and science experiences yield a practice of science that one might expect wherever science gets done: They ask questions and find ways to solve them. They draw on their own intuitive understandings and creative powers alongside the knowledge and experiences of experts. They seek answers that have meaning in their lives. On the other hand, their lives give witness to a particular enactment of science—one that calls attention to their hopes and dreams for themselves and their communities as well as to the myriad ways in which their hopes and dreams have been challenged by a society often blind to the struggles of poor children. The stories are embedded with rage and hope, with joys and fears, with dreams for a better tomorrow for both themselves and their communities. In short, the science practices of their lives, although qualitatively not too different from the work that scientists do in the most general sense, reflect ways of being that may provide potential insight into how we might build bridges between science and youth.

is our hope that the stories we tell here capture the power and beauty of the narratives and experiences that the youth have shared with us. In short, what we hope that the readers gain from reading this text is an understanding of which science experiences are relevant to youth living in urban poverty and why they are so. In showing which science experiences are relevant, we also work to demonstrate how power, authority, identity, and action all play pivotal roles in the sense that youth make of their lives and in their attempts to use science (in part) to craft empowering opportunities to have their needs addressed. Although the stories show that doing science is far from the "central activity" in these youth's lives either in or out of school, they also show that youth often take advantage of the opportunities they have for doing science to gain power and control in their lives.

WHY USE YOUTH STORIES TO MAKE A CASE FOR URBAN SCIENCE EDUCATION?

Children in poverty constitute 26% of the urban population, yet account for 41% of the high-poverty urban population, with more than 50% of urban children hovering near the federal poverty line at some time in their lives[2] (Dalaker, 2001; U.S. Department of Education, 1996). Almost 17% of the nation's students live in poverty, but in major cities, such as New York, Los Angeles, Atlanta, and New Orleans, the percentages hover around 35–45% (National Center for Education Statistics, 2002). In fact, more than 40% of urban students attend high-poverty schools (U.S. Department of Education, 1996). While White children constitute the majority of the poor in absolute numbers, children from Hispanic and African American families are overrepresented in poverty statistics and in particular in urban poverty statistics, with the urban poverty rates of Hispanic and African American families more than triple than that of White families (U.S. Census Bureau, 2001).[3] The numbers of children living in extreme poverty are also staggering—more than 2 million people experienced homelessness at some point during the calendar year, with nearly half that population being children (National Law Center on Homelessness and Poverty, 2000).

Although poignant, these statistics leave us with many unanswered questions. Who exactly are these children living in urban poverty? What are their experiences? What are their stories? There are many stories that can be told—and that have been told—about high-poverty, urban children's experiences. As the statistics above suggest, the great majority of these stories are quantitative in nature.[4] Indeed, over the past 10 years, the science education community has supported studies that document divisions in

academic achievement, resources, and schooling practices that di
ate the educational experiences of high-poverty, urban youth fror.
of their more affluent and suburban counterparts. These studies reve ., .or
example, that high-poverty urban youth score lower on standardized tests;
have decreased access to rigorous courses, books, scientific equipment,
compensatory programs, or qualified teachers; and drop out of school at
higher rates than those of their more affluent and suburban counterparts
(Anyon, 1997; Council of the Great City Schools, 1994; Darling-Hammond,
1999; Education Trust, 1996; Fine, 1991; Ingersoll, 1999; Oakes, 1990; Oakes,
Gamoran, & Page, 1992; Oakes, Muir, & Joseph, 2000). These quantitative
findings have been and continue to be important: They teach us about the
kinds of spaces that mark inequitable opportunities for high-poverty,
urban youth. They show us the impact these inequalities have on students'
achievement and attitudes in a broad fashion. They point toward the kinds
of things the science education community might begin to do differently
in its research and teaching efforts.

Yet we also know from our own experiences doing science with children and youth in urban poverty that these stories help us to understand
only pieces of youth's lives. We also need to understand the narrative
wholes in which the pieces are embedded in ways that accentuate what
high-poverty, urban youth already bring to the practice of science. For the
most part, the quantitative stories presented in the works cited earlier focus
on what high-poverty, urban youth lack (as compared to what their more
affluent and suburban counterparts are able to obtain). This is only one
piece of the picture. In this book, we make the claim that we must build on
this research around urban science education with rich, contextual stories
of the lives of youth, because these stories will begin to put faces to the
issues and begin to illuminate the positive and consequential aspects of their
lives, aspects that are crucial to our work in science education and schooling. Witherell and Noddings (1991) make just this point in their argument
about the stories that lives tell:

> Stories are powerful research tools. They provide us with a picture of real
> people in real situations, struggling with real problems. They banish the in-
> difference often generated by samples, treatments and faceless subjects. They
> invite us to speculate on what might be changed and with what effect.
> (p. 280)

Much has been written on the power of stories in educational research.
Hutchinson (1999) uses the phrase "core story" to distinguish meaningful
stories, which can take a variety of formats, from those of the more traditional story form, which "may or may not carry significant meaning"

(p. 76). She argues that for stories to have meaning in teaching and educational research, they must report more than a listing of dates, places, and events. They must also speak to the meaning of those events in an individual's life. In the tradition developed and expanded by Clandinin and Connelly (2000), Casey (1993), Witherell and Noddings (1991), McAdams (1993) and Hutchinson (1999), we also use qualitative stories to develop rich, contextual, narrative accounts of lives. We further draw on the tradition of narrative inquiry, life history, and story-based research and expand our argument about the importance of stories in urban science education to make the claim that stories of the lives of youth are central to our understandings of science education practices because they are contextual, situated, political, whole, meaningful, and protean.

In reflecting on stories as meaning over stories as fact, what we see as important is that the stories themselves become a piece of history, a lens through which to interpret which features of that context have significance for the author, and in what ways and through what connections (Personal Narratives Group, 1989). In this sense, stories pull together an understanding of personal identity and cultural context that allow us "to counteract cultural givens which may otherwise dominate expressions of one's life" (Hutchinson, 1999, p. 92). Hutchinson (1999) makes a case for why stories as meaning are ethically and psychologically just as important as stories as description of fact:

> I recall a young third grade girl who stole small items from her teacher's purse. Knowing only the facts of this case, that the girl actually stole items, would do little to understand or help this child. This child would simply be punished or suspended from school. Perhaps from an institutional or legal perspective, she should. Yet understanding the possible meaning of why she did these acts might lead one to make a different judgment. (p. 85)

Thus, the importance of stories is not the accuracy of the stories, per se, but in the meaning it has for both the teller and the reader.

Stories are also protean and underscore human agency (Delgado-Gaitan, 1996; Delgado-Gaitan & Trueba, 1991; Hutchinson, 1999). Not only do stories actively position youth as creators of their own lives, they also are always embedded in and change along with the communities which sustain or challenge them (Goodson, 1992). The transformational nature of stories works along many directions. The meanings to be garnered from the stories of youth change as the reader changes. The same story may carry different meanings because of one's social or political position, occupation, or life experiences. Stories can also transform the reader. Because stories allow youth's voices—voices typically absent in educational research—to enter mainstream science education discourse, we are granted opportunities to be presented with and changed by their experiences and worldviews.

For example, initially, we did not understand the tunnel under the fence as science or even as an event of particular importance to our efforts in the after-school science program. After all, the children were not trying to determine the best way to dig tunnels, nor were they studying anything, really, about the process of digging a tunnel. Furthermore, their tunnel was not connected to our study of butterfly life cycles or the local ecology that guided our work that semester. Our initial reaction was that the children were simply being mischievous. However, once we listened to their stories and realized that they had studied a problem (not having a place to play), came up with a solution (dig a tunnel under the fence), then went in search of ways to enact their solution (use the leftover wood from the bird feeders, pretend the hole was dug by an animal, dig it wide and shallow to accommodate Texas soil and in a location where no one would notice), we began to see how our own understandings of the purposes and products of scientific activity were limited. Digging a tunnel under a fence was just as important (if not more so) than building a butterfly garden, and it posed a much greater design problem. By opening ourselves to their story, we began to see that we could not just label as scientific only those things *we* saw as scientific. We had to allow our understanding of what they were doing to be transformed. We also had to allow our understanding of the purpose of doing or learning science at that particular juncture to be transformed.

We are not saying that the mere act of digging a tunnel was science or even that it measured up against anything we might teach them. We would be fooling ourselves to believe that "anything goes." Simply digging a tunnel is not necessarily science. We are also not saying that we believe it necessary to follow up their actions with a unit on building tunnels. This is much too superficial a connection. However, carefully listening to the youth tell their story about the tunnel, we began to see how they applied a scientific mindset to solving their problem. Being more attentive to their actions, we gained a better sense of the questions that mattered to them and of the ways in which they activated different resources to answer those questions. For example, we began to see that there were many avenues we could pursue. From this one story we learned something about power and control—that rules youth perceived as unfair matter enough to be challenged and could provide a unique lens for analyzing our own decisions as teachers. Is the student resistance we sometimes experience a result of students not wanting to do the science we planned or of poorly conceived class-management strategies? Could we or should we also consider some of the assumptions we bring to "following rules" in order to make sense of why some science activities work and others do not?

We also learned something about the areas of science that might interest youth—that youth have experience and interest in building tools from readily available materials. We could have, for example, followed up later with a unit on tool design. Scientists commonly design their own tools when what they have at their disposal does not fit their problem at the moment.

Finally, we learned about social relations and identity. Although many of the youth in our research oftentimes had difficulty working in groups, with children of different ages or grade levels, or in coeducational settings, they created a situation on their own in which such boundaries were crossed and in which such boundary crossing appeared to be necessary. Learning about how and when youth find or create the occasion to cross these boundaries is also an important part of science teaching.

For us, as teachers and researchers, being open to youth's stories helped us to grow in our thinking about how science and the lives of youth might intersect in powerful learning moments. We believe that this kind of change on our part is important because it helped us to see beyond our own stories to better understand youth's lives.

In the stories in this book, we aim to present youth and the practices in science they construct in holistic, authentic, and active ways. The stories draw from the composite of qualities of stories described earlier to describe to others the lives and the science experiences, beliefs, concerns, and needs of youth who are living and learning in urban poverty. As we outline in the following section, some of these stories are about the youth themselves, while others are about the teaching of youth.

LEARNING IN CONTEXT

It is important to begin stories of youth's lives and youth's science with a discussion of context because it helps to set the stage for understanding how the landscape in which science occurs is contested. The landscape is not simply a location such as a classroom or a shelter, but rather is composed of many different forms of power and knowledge that make up the practice of science, including questions about not just the spaces where science gets done, but also the lives of those who do the science, the science itself, and the cultural and political terrain in which such events occur (McLaren, 1992).

There are two contexts that drive most of the stories in this book—Southside Shelter in New York City and Hope Shelter in central Texas. Although descriptions of these contexts emerge in the stories presented in this text, we provide a summary description of these contexts in what follows.

Life at Southside Shelter in New York City

Although family homelessness has been a part of New York City's land-scape since the city was founded, it was not recognized as a public issue until the 1980s (Beard, 1987). Since the 1980s, homelessness has increased more than 500% and has disproportionately affected children and people of color (Homes for the Homeless [HFH], 2001). The average homeless person in New York City is a single mother of two children, in her late 20s, and unemployed and who has had at least one public assistance cut within the past year (HFH, 2001). Children from homeless families constitute two thirds of all homeless individuals and disproportionately suffer from a lack of adequate healthcare, educational deprivation, social stigma, and weak social circles. In fact, homeless children develop chronic respiratory infec-tions, gastrointestinal diseases, ear disorders, and dermatological problems at a rate double that of "homed" poor urban children (National Center for Health Statistics, 1995).[5] Furthermore, one in five homeless families has one or more children in foster care (HFH, 2001). This is a rate much higher than that for homed families, for whom the social service emphasis is more likely to be on working closely with the families to help them address underly-ing problems that put their children at risk rather than on punishing the family by taking children away, as is the case with homeless families.

Conservative public and social policies have not met the needs of home-less families and in fact have contributed to the increase in the number of homeless families in New York City and nationwide.[6] Cuts in federal and state assistance to the poor have destabilized families such that the leading housing emergencies historically (fires, hazardous living conditions, personal calamities) no longer constitute the primary cause of family homelessness (HFH, 2001). Both working and nonworking families have been forced to abandon their homes. According to de Nunez (1995), systematic reductions in programs that serve the urban poor has led to the "notching down" of an entire generation into a chronic and debilitating poverty that claims home-lessness as one of its most defining characteristics.

Southside Shelter, built in 1997, is a relatively new family homeless shelter in the Top Hill neighborhood of New York City. Since the late 1800s, Top Hill has been home to many different immigrant populations: Irish, Jewish, Italian, Russian, African, and Caribbean. As each ethnic group made its way into the predominant U.S. culture, it moved from Top Hill to more affluent suburbs, for example, on Long Island, in New Jersey, and in the northern Bronx. However, in the 1970s these dynamics changed. Many of the Black families chose to stay in the neighborhood, in part because they were not as welcome in the more traditional "stepping stone" communi-ties as were other, White ethnic groups, in part because their economic success had not mirrored that of the previous (White) ethnic groups to inhabit Top Hill.

Top Hill is home mainly to Black and Latino/a populations. There are significant Puerto Rican and multigenerational Black populations, as well as a large population of recent immigrants to the United States from places like the Dominican Republic, the West Indies, Mexico, and Africa. Many turf wars now take place in Top Hill between recent immigrants (mainly Latino/a) and the multigenerational Black community members. There are even turf wars among the highly diverse Latino/a populations, with Puerto Rican and Dominican Republic families often claiming dominance over those from their poorer Central American neighbors, such as El Salvador, Guatemala, and Nicaragua. As these turf wars suggest, Top Hill can be a tough place in which to live.

After having experienced economic decline in the 1970s and 1980s, Top Hill was just beginning to recover during the economic boom of the 1990s in the United States. There are several bodegas, check-cashing stores, and fast-food restaurants lining the streets. However, the neighborhood is mainly home to towering residential apartments, boarded-up buildings, abandoned lots, and a large comprehensive high school. A walk around the neighborhood reveals that although the streets teem with adolescent life, they also tend to be littered with garbage and dog feces. The kinds of city-sponsored cleanup efforts seen on Manhattan's Upper East Side are not a part of Top Hill's reality.

Additionally, Top Hill has a long history of gang- and drug-related activity. Not many weeks pass when one doesn't hear about gang-related violence that has ended in the death of or severe injury to a young person. In fact, this neighborhood has been depicted in a negative manner in the local and national media, and residents of other parts of the city often refer to this neighborhood as undesirable and dangerous. Even though crime statistics in New York City as a whole steadily decreased between 1992 and 2002, there has actually been an increase in violent crime in the Top Hill and surrounding neighborhoods.

Southside Shelter is one of the largest family shelters in the city. It is sandwiched between a large comprehensive high school with a reputation of ranking below the city and state average in test scores and a city park known for its violence. Southside is different from many other shelters in the city because it serves all kinds of families, whereas many of the family shelters are strictly earmarked for individuals suffering from domestic abuse, drug-related homelessness, or HIV/AIDS. Southside is run by a private organization that receives private, federal, state, and local funding to sustain its operations in order to serve people displaced from their permanent residences. The purpose of these shelters is to enable homeless individuals to find permanent housing and along the way find employment or obtain skills that will allow them to sustain permanent housing. The founders of Southside pride themselves on their commitment to "living for today and building for tomorrow." They believe that their multifaceted approach to homeless families (education and job training, housing, and counseling) will help their families assimilate more easily and more quickly into society, becoming self-sufficient.

The shelter itself is well kept and simultaneously resembles a motor lodge that one might see on an interstate freeway and a prison (depending on who is asked). It is a two-winged, four-story complex painted burnt orange and has a playground for young children. The whole complex is walled off from the rest of the neighborhood by a large black metal fence encapsulating the structure on all four sides. The buildings that house the residents are constructed of cinder block. Some residents have complained that this structure leaves them cold in the winter and able to hear their neighbors. Upon entering a unit, one can clearly make out the unfinished cinder block walls. Each unit has its own kitchenette, bathroom, living room area, and bedroom area. However, except for the bathrooms, there are no formal dividing partitions in the units. The main entrance to the shelter has a check-in desk and waiting area like that of a motel or a prison. This shelter also serves as a working facility, with administrative offices, recreation rooms, a computer room, a conference room, a maintenance department, day care, and preschool programs for children between the ages of 2½ and 5 years old. There are on-site social workers, counselors, GED programs, school-age children's programs, and city administrators.

Life at Hope Shelter in Central Texas

Hope Shelter is located in Well Springs, Texas, a southwestern urban center, known for its recent economic boom and population expansion. Its population now ranks it as one of the 20 largest cities in the United States. This population explosion has had a devastating impact on the working poor in Well Springs. The housing and rental markets are so saturated that affordable housing is nonexistent. More than 10,000 school-age children (K-12) are homeless in Well Springs over the course of a school year, and a significant percentage of these children are from working families who simply cannot afford the rising cost of living.[7]

Well Springs is for the most part a segregated city, with most of the families of color (mainly Mexican American and Black families) living on the east side of the city. East and west Well Springs are clearly demarcated by a major double-decker highway that runs through the city, limiting points of crossing and even views of "the other side." The city offers more social services than other cities in the state, but compared to those of cities outside Texas, such as New York City, these services are severely limited. In Well Springs' shelters, there are only enough beds to cover $1/10$ of the homeless population in the city, and unless families and children can document "legal residence" in the country, they are denied access to services.

Hope Shelter, built in 1996, sits on the outskirts of Well Springs. The rationale behind its construction so far from the heartbeat of the city was admirable: The land was cheaper, allowing the organization to provide families more on its limited budget, and the organization believed that such a distant location would keep the residents safer. This location, however, has created its own set of problems. Most mothers who live at Hope work in the service industry, and thus their jobs take them into the heart of the city. As in most southwestern cities, public transportation is limited to a bus system that is already taxed, in this case by the growing population in Well Springs. Several mothers have explained to us that they travel almost 2 hours each way to get from the shelter to their minimum-wage jobs in motels and stores—commutes that would take only 20 to 30 minutes by car.

Hope Shelter provides both short- and long-term housing for women and children who are in economic hardship and who are the survivors of domestic abuse. Hope's newly constructed short-term housing facilities, built in 2000, serve families who are the immediate escapees of domestic violence. Stays in short-term housing are limited to 6 weeks, and while living there, mothers and children receive extensive support services and counseling from Hope staff. Adjacent to the short-term buildings are Hope's long-term, or "supportive housing," facilities, which provide housing to families for, on average, 12 to 15 months. In supportive housing, Hope serves approximately 70 families and is home to more than 100 children, one third of whom are school-aged. Demographically, at any given time, approximately half the residents are Latina/o (predominately Mexican American), one quarter are Black, and one quarter are White.

As mentioned in the "tunnel story," which opened this chapter, physically, the grounds of Hope Shelter are surrounded by a large, black security fence, which in certain sections is topped with barbed wire. Interior fences surround and separate the short-term and supportive housing facilities. The fences also separate the housing spaces from play spaces—grassy areas and playground—and severely limit children's playtime to the immediate after-school hours.

Shared Contexts

Although there are many commonalties between the contexts and experiences of the children and youth living at Southside and those of the young residents at Hope, as the preceding descriptions indicate, there are three parallels in context of particular importance.

First, locating and keeping a residence at Southside or Hope, as at other city shelters in both Texas and New York, is riddled with bureaucratic red tape and games of chance for the youth and their families. Families have to prove legal residence in the United States. They must show that they have no assistance from other family members in the same city, even if they may be estranged from those family members. They have to prove marriage if both parents are moving into a shelter. This is often a dehumanizing process. Some youth described sleeping on the floors in the offices of social workers while awaiting assistance. Other described having to witness their parents beg for help when assistance was not forthcoming. Still other children described going through the shelter housing application process many times before being granted housing. One mother described this process of forcing individuals to apply and reapply for assistance as the city's way of wearing down the poor to the point where they have to literally beg for help.

Second, as the tunnel story suggests, the physical structure of the shelter contributes to the children and youth feeling contained, overly regulated, and without much personal space. Many of the youth who live at Southside, like the children at Hope, believed that the shelter rules along with its physical construction give the shelter a prisonlike or cagelike feel, as shown in this interview of Shorty, 13 years old, conducted by Darkside, age 15:

> DARKSIDE: What are some words that you use to describe living in a homeless shelter?
> SHORTY: Oh. What kind of words? OK, it's boring. It sucks. Ain't nothing to do. It feel like you locked in a cage.
> DARKSIDE: It feel like you on lockdown. They got you on lockdown or somethin'.
> SHORTY: You have a curfew. You have to be signed in and out.
> DARKSIDE: Yes, you have to sign in and out.
> SHORTY: And I'm not used to that.
> DARKSIDE: I'm not used to it neither but that's just the rules.

Darkside, who is a Black Cuban American, and Shorty, who is African American, agree that these rules make it "feel like you on lockdown." However, as both teens suggest, they recognize that these are just the rules, and as Darkside describes it later in that same conversation, "It's better than having your head in the street." Thus, although the youth feel locked down by these rules, they are grateful for their shelter. Additionally, the majority of the youth are embarrassed to have their friends find out that they live at a shelter, as Kobe (a 16-year-old African American) described:

> I don't like [my high school] because, you know, it's too close to home. And the friends I might make there might live around the way, which they sure enough do. They might laugh at where I live.

Third, and similar to the second point, the shelter system restricts autonomy. Both Southside and Hope, like most other shelter systems, are highly regulated. Both shelters sport a sign-in desk upon one's entering the shelter through the front gate (again, in both places, the only entrance). Southside's entry way was even monitored by two security guards. At both locations all visitors and shelter residents must sign in and out at the front desk and show picture identification before being allowed to enter the premises. At Southside, adult residents may not stay out past 10 P.M., teenage children may not "hang out" around the building, and young children cannot run around in the playground unless supervised by adults. Additionally, in neither location can residents have guests, even if these guests are family members—whether mothers, grandmothers, or children—or friends. Infractions of these rules along with violations of drug use, domestic violence, child abuse, or any other criminal activity often resulted in immediate eviction or discharge from the facility.

LOOKING AHEAD: THE STORIES IN THIS TEXT

Clearly, the circumstances that surround the lives of youth living in urban poverty present them with obstacles in the form of rules and regulations, material conditions, and social expectations and stereotypes that work to limit their success and potential inside and outside school. Yet, as the story about the tunnel suggests, children are resourceful, resilient, and able to make the best out of what resources they have access to.

The first three chapters establish a foundation for the stories and ideas presented in this book, including a discussion of what it means to learn about a practice of science from children and youth living and learning in urban poverty. In Chapter 2, we weave together a discussion of what we mean by "a practice of science" and its importance in youth lives along with our theoretical framework (a critical/feminist stance on schooling, culture, and science), and an overview of the methods and contexts. Chapter 3, "Living in the Borderland," focuses more closely on what it means to live in urban poverty. In this chapter, we tell the stories of two youth, Claudia and Juan, and use their stories to raise questions and issues related to living and learning in the borderland. Drawing from feminist theories, we show how the students in our study find strength—political and ideological—by carefully and critically understanding how society supports separations between individuals and groups of individuals based on race, ethnicity, social class, and gender.

Chapters 4 through 8 present a series of "youth lives and youth science" stories. Almost, but not all, of these stories are taken from our teaching and researching in after-school science programs with children and youth in homeless shelters in central Texas and in New York City. Those stories that are not taken from the after-school programs are culled from our conversations and observations of youth while we were just hanging out with them, from the stories they have told us, and from our observations of them in schools. The reasons for telling these stories are twofold. First, we share in rich, contextual detail the lives of youth living in urban poverty so that the reader can have the opportunity to get to know the youth and have a context for making sense of what it means to grow up impoverished in an urban setting and what it means to move in and out of homeless situations. All the youth whose stories are shared here have experienced homelessness and have lived in homeless shelters for time periods ranging from 6 months to 4 years. Our second reason for telling these stories is to share the science practices the youth actively construct in their lives. These stories are presented to begin to make a coherent case for what it means for youth living in urban poverty to construct a practice of science.

In Chapter 4, "Power and Co-opting Science Spaces," we examine the first cross-cutting theme we use to describe a practice of science: power and co-opting science spaces. We present two different case studies of Mexican American youth, and we respond to the following two questions: In what ways do youth interact with science in their lives, both in and out of school? How do power relations frame these interactions? In this chapter, we take a close look at the power issues that frame the youth's lives and at how youth actively use science to transform those power relations. We examine two themes along the lines of transforming power: disrupting structures and disrupting identities and relationships. We use these two themes to argue that youth adopt science spaces for multiple purposes and they use their authority to challenge the ways of knowing in school science and the culture of power that sustains those practices. We argue that knowing both "sides"—how to critique or challenge science and how to become part of science and then using that knowledge to one's benefit—are central to youth's practices of science.

In Chapter 5, "Relevant Science: Activating Resources in Nonstandard Ways," we reflect on the following question: What makes science relevant or responsive to youth's lives? In this chapter, we write about the desire among the youth to make science something that is their own—something that reflects who they are and who they want to be—and how they creatively use the resources to which they have access.

In Chapter 6, "Transformations: Science as a Tool for Change," we build on the ideas of "co-opting science" and "activating nonstandard resources" to show how youth use their practices of science to bring about change in their lives and in their worlds. In presenting one story in detail, that of Darkside and the community garden, we make a case for how doing science and working together to make changes in the community are intertwined in the ideal of using science as a formative tool for generating personal and community change. By illustrating how science brings about different kinds of change, we make the claim that all teaching and learning science is political. This stance about science raises the question, How might science education programs be built on the values of a socially just and democratic society?

In Chapter 7, "Building Communities in Support of Youth's Science Practices," we explore how youth understand and build communities that are supportive of their science practices. We use the youth's experiences to raise a set of key teaching dilemmas around the following aspects of community: building a community around real science, a desire for inclusiveness, and a responsiveness to the urban context.

In Chapter 8, "Empowering Science Education and Youth's Practices of Science," we return to the questions that have guided us: What concerns do young people living in urban poverty have, and how does this influence their practices of science? How might the science teaching practice we construct formally, in school and out of school, with young people in urban poverty reflect their lives, their concerns, and their practices of science? Our return to these questions is marked by our efforts not to answer them definitively, but to better understand what the questions might mean for us as teachers and researchers in high-poverty, urban settings. We situate these reflections in the stories and ideas presented in the first seven chapters, the literature around education for social justice, and our own desire to craft teaching practices that promote global sustainability. As Peter McLaren reminds us, "The wealth of our nation (and of the nations of the world) should be measured by the elimination of class exploitation, racism, sexism, homophobia, and other forms of oppression, by the health of a people, their creative capacities, their standard of living and their well-being" (in Calabrese Barton, 2001, p. 13). We believe strongly that unless and until an approach to science and science education in our urban classrooms focuses on what it might mean to create a more just world, then we will fall short of our goal of truly building a science education for all.

CHAPTER 2

Learning with Urban Youth

This chapter establishes a foundation for the stories and ideas presented in this book, including a discussion of what it means to learn about a practice of science from students living and learning in urban poverty. In establishing this foundation, we weave together a discussion of our theoretical framework (a critical/feminist stance on schooling, culture, and science), with an overview of the methods and contexts that drive our work. In the final section of this chapter we present an analytic framework for understanding youth's practices of science.

THE CONTRADICTIONS OF DOING SCIENCE IN AND OUT OF SCHOOL: KOBE'S STORY

Kobe was a tall, handsome, dark-skinned "16-going-on-17" year old African American young man. He walked with a pronounced swagger characteristic of many of his peers and exuded a cool confidence. During the time I (Angie) worked with Kobe, he carefully burned a gang identity symbol into the top of his left hand, which he often hid inside his oversized Starter jacket.

Kobe lived at Southside Shelter in New York City with his mother, 1-year-old sister, and 2-year-old and 9-year-old brothers. His only older brother was "in jail down south." He couldn't wait to grow up and move out and be on his own, because he wanted privacy and personal time. This was not surprising given that Kobe often had primary child-care responsibilities for his siblings. Kobe's mother, for various reasons, would sneak out of the shelter (against shelter regulations) for days at a time, leaving Kobe to care for his siblings. When this happened Kobe made sure his siblings were fed and in bed at a reasonable hour, although he was not so intent on making sure his 9-year-old brother got to school.

Kobe was an intensely private—but not shy—young man. He talked a great deal about sports, music, and clubs but rarely let me, or others, into his private life. In fact, I had known Kobe for more than 2 months before I found out he was the primary caregiver for his siblings—and when I did find out it was by accident. He had missed a scheduled meeting with me and so I had gone up to his unit to see if he was home and still interested in meeting. He stuck his head out of the door, keeping both the door and his body as a defense against me entering or seeing inside his unit, and asked if I could wait another hour. When I returned an hour later, I found him in the kitchen with a loaf of bread in one hand, a baby on one hip, and another young child sitting on the bed in the kitchen, crying. It was then that I learned about his mother's frequent absences and his responsibility for his siblings.

Kobe's deep level of commitment to those around him was evident in other ways. He was committed to his gang, serving often as their "eyes" in various kinds of exchanges. He was also committed to his close personal friends. He could often be found in a particularly close friend's unit talking with her or out in the courtyard watching her son. He had a difficult time with drugs; he was often high on pot or crack.

Kobe left school in the early fall of his sophomore year, although he did not officially drop out of school. Schooling was difficult at best: he found school boring and had developed an adversarial relationship with several of his teachers:

> Well really, my science teacher, the row that I'm in, and some of the girls, and some of the kids, you know, they think they run things up in there. So, and what else. It's like, you know . . . I hate it that I don't do my work. Because, oh yeah, my teacher, I hate her. Last year, she failed me because I was gonna pass her class with a 65, she failed me because I said, "If you bring your Lexus to school, I'll stab your tires."

According to Kobe, school did not matter anyway because he planned a future in sports, and he preferred to play on a community team over his school team:

> I'm smart, I'm real smart. They just think 'cause I always slack around and play too much, you know, and get high and drunk. No. I don't play [basketball] for my school, because you know, my school is, how do you say, *garbage* (drawn out and exaggerated).

Kobe planned for a future centered on sports. He had picked the pseudonym Kobe for himself because of the basketball star Kobe Bryant. He planned to make it big in basketball, but if basketball did not work out he was willing to try football and even baseball. If sports in general did not work out, Kobe wanted to become a chef:

> [What I want from life is] basically as everyone, grow and die, but be rich and have grandkids. Lots and lots of grandkids. But, you know, I wanna become an NBA star or an NFL star. If that doesn't work, I don't want to try it, but if I have to, baseball, 'cause I'm real good. But, I don't like it. I mean I like it though and, you know, what else? Um, what else do I wanna do? And a job, and if that doesn't work out? The athlete's thing, become a cook, a chef, 'cause I can really cook. But this is my interview. But I wanna be a cook, 'cause I can cook. I can throw down in the kitchen.

Although Kobe had not been attending school, he did participate in the after-school science program at Southside Shelter. His participation was sparse at first. While many of Kobe's peers at the shelter were involved in the project to convert an abandoned lot into a community garden, Kobe only watched from a distance, often ridiculing his peers about their wasting their efforts on a project that would never succeed. Several months into the project, we began to interview the teens about their experiences in transforming the lot. Kobe often came to these interviews (at the invitation of his friends), listening in from the side, and eventually expressing an interest in being interviewed and in designing and conducting interviews. I immediately responded to his interest because I wanted to involve Kobe in ways that were meaningful to him. He had not participated in the project thus far, and most of his conversation had focused on why the lot transformation would be unsuccessful. Because participation in the "research" aspect of the project (the interviews) required parental consent, I went with Kobe to his unit to talk to his mother about his participation. On the way to his unit, Kobe asked me if he could carry the camera. When I told him that that was fine, we shared the following exchange:

> KOBE: How do you know I won't break it? Or steal it?
> ANGIE: I don't.
> KOBE: How do you know I won't hurt you?
> ANGIE: I don't. How do you know I won't hurt you?
> KOBE: I don't.

Although this conversation transpired more than 3 years ago, it still feels to me as if it were yesterday. So much was embedded in this short exchange over the camera. On the one hand, Kobe towered at least an entire foot over me. His figure was lanky as is true for many tall teenage boys, but he was athletically fit and physically aggressive. On the other hand, as an educated middle-class White woman, I carried with me the capital of being White in America.

The interviews drew Kobe into an ongoing debate with his peers about the purposes, goals, and importance of the lot transformation project. He took these interviews rather seriously, challenging his peers to support their claims about the importance of the lot transformation project, as this extended quote suggests:

> KOBE: Really, you know . . . I don't like talkin' about the community. Related to science, you know, I just don't like that lot that we have across the street 'cause, you know, it's all garbage and I don't know why they try to fix it up. It's gonna stay an empty lot. All that's gonna be there is the same junk there is now.
>
> STEVE: Um, Kobe, like, how come you don't get hope again? Yeah.
>
> KOBE: Because, I mean look at it. I mean, who's really gonna be here? Who's really gonna spend their time over there workin' and, and it's built on a sewer. I mean, not a sewer. What do you call it? A (*pause*), a swamp. And all these rats, people have little children runnin' around here, man. They could seriously get bit, or hurt you know. Excuse me.
>
> STEVE: Okay, Kobe. Got kinda touchy there, but see, I don't agree with you 'cause people might get hope in that lot. And they might build something good on there. So what's your thoughts?
>
> KOBE: But, you can't put, you can't build, well you can build, but you just can't build concrete, because, you know, it will collapse, and then the sewage stuff. Stuff like that. So, all right. There you go.
>
> STEVE: But we could do the garden or a playground or something—
>
> KOBE: (*Interrupting*) Now see, for order you to build a playground, you need concrete. You know? All right, how you expect the swings to stay on . . . to stay down into the dirt?
>
> STEVE: On the spongy mats, you know—
>
> KOBE: (*Interrupting*) But I'm sayin'. Like I said, those you call the spongy mats, right, well one day I might, you know. Well you know, it's like a bad neigh—you know kids drive by you know, throwin' things out they car, bottles. It might hit the building and cut a kid. All right?
>
> STEVE: You do got a point, but you know, we gonna build a fence around it. And like, we gonna have securities on it—
>
> KOBE: (*Interrupting*) But, excuse me, like I said, they drive by and throw bottles and stuff like that out their window. How is a

security guard gonna stop them from doing that while they're just standing there, in a car, they're in a car! How are they gonna stop them? And you know, like I was sayin', and what's that fence gonna do? They say, like I said (*pause*) the fence could hit the build—I mean the gate—the bottle could hit the building behind the fence, and the fence doesn't stop glass from going through the little holes in the fence really. It doesn't really help, you know.

STEVE: Again, you got a point, but . . . (*changes the subject*)

Kobe's participation in the interviews slowly introduced him to the other youth and their involvement in the science project, and as a consequence, his participation spread to other aspects of the project. He became one of three coproducers/codirectors of a video made by teens for teens about life and science in the inner city (*The Urban Atmosphere*). He also began to participate in the garden project. He helped with cleaning the lot and with planting the vegetables. And through his debates, helped to sharpen the plans for future activity.

Kobe's participation in the after-school science project, as an interviewer, filmmaker, and garden helper, greatly affected him. In the late spring, Kobe came to the decision that he would go back to school on the days he could. He hoped he might salvage something from his sophomore year, and he decided that if sports did not work out, he might have science as a backup career. Kobe reported his experience of returning to school to me with harsh language and deep emotion. As his story goes, the first class he returned to was science. He felt that he had "learned a little with the lot project" and thought this would be the "place" to go back. However, when he entered his class, his teacher asked him who he was in front of the rest of the students. When he stated his name and how he had been enrolled in the course, the teacher said he didn't remember him, laughed, and informed him that it was too late for him to try to pass the semester. The rest of the students laughed as well. Kobe left school after class and did not return for the rest of the school year. As he later stated to me: "I was going to have science as a backup career, but now, no. No. I try to do the right thing and go back to school, and what do I get? Just the reason why I left. No respect."

SCIENCE FOR ALL: THE ISSUES THAT DIVIDE

A Critical Perspective on Science Education in Urban Settings

We begin with a story about Kobe because it exposes the contradictions emergent in his own school and science lives. This story shows Kobe caring for his siblings, challenging his peers' thinking, and engaging in scientific practice in his local community. Yet this same story also shows him missing months and months of school science, threatening his freshman year science teacher physically, and experiencing a level of harassment in school that ultimately fueled his decision to leave school altogether. These same contradictions between the strengths that youth bring to school and to science and how it is that those in powerful positions (teachers, researchers, and policy makers) neglect to see those strengths because of an overt attention to youth's deficits also mark our research efforts in science education.

A brief, summative review of the urban science education literature, including the recent reform initiatives (herein referred to as science for all), draws our attention, for the most part, to what is it that urban youth *lack* in terms of achievement, resources, and educative opportunities.[1]

The literature on achievement and urban youth focuses mainly on the statistical analyses that show that children and youth in high-poverty, urban settings are quantitatively lagging behind their more affluent and suburban counterparts. High-poverty, urban children score disproportionately low on standardized tests and on school grades in the sciences and science-related areas, and fewer than half of urban students are above national achievement norms (Council of the Great City Schools, 2001). Impoverished, urban children drop out of school at rates significantly higher than those of more affluent children, with impoverished and urban Black and Hispanic children having the highest drop-out rates in the United States (Fine, 1991). Fewer than half the ninth graders in central city schools complete high school in 4 years (Education Trust, 1996). In fact, the national policy trend in education in the United States—to add new layers of testing to document failure in order to "close down" low performing schools— is squarely situated in deficit thinking.

The research around the issue of resources shows a similarly negative trend. Research to date demonstrates that children attending high-poverty, urban schools have reduced access to new textbooks, scientific equipment, and science-related extracurricular activities (Oakes, 1990; Oakes et al., 2000). They also have limited access to certified math and science teachers or to administrators who support high-quality science teaching (Ingersoll, 1999). Impoverished urban districts, such as some districts in New York City and Los Angeles, support a teaching force in which the percentage of uncertified and unqualified science teachers outweighs the percentage of certified and qualified teachers (Darling-Hammond, 1999). Urban students in high-poverty schools or schools with high minority enrollment have limited access to high-level math and science courses (Oakes et al., 2000) and are disproportionately tracked into low-level classes in which educational achievement typically focuses on behavior skills and static conceptions of knowledge (Oakes, Gamoran, & Page, 1992). Further, in these classes students spend more time reading from textbooks and completing worksheets and are expected to be passive learners rather than active users and producers of disciplinary knowledge. Some studies have even shown a complete absence of science in these low-track classes (Page, 1989, 1990).

We suppose it is no wonder that the vast majority of urban students lose interest in and develop relatively negative attitudes toward science by the time they complete the middle grades (Hill, Atwater, & Wiggins, 1995). The research shows that students living and learning in urban poverty have inequitable access to the kinds of science classes, teachers, resources, and opportunities necessary for their academic success in science. It also shows that the challenges in urban science education are layered and these layers are deeply connected to one another and to issues of power and control.

The science education reform efforts that mark the past 15 years and that have been supported by both the National Research Council (NRC, 1996) and the American Association for the Advancement of Science (AAAS, 1989) attempt to confront these issues that cause divisions. In science education reform policy and practice circles, K–12 schools, and teacher education programs, we often hear the phrase "scientific literacy for all." While most science educators in Western nations refer to key policy documents such as AAAS's Project 2061 (AAAS, 1989), UNESCO's *Project 2000+* (1993), and the Science Research Council of Canada's *Science for Every Citizen* (1984) to justify and explain the importance of scientific literacy for all, some have also drawn on historical accounts of the call for "science for all," such as Wilkinson's 1847 lecture titled *Science for All*. The general focus in these early calls for widespread science literacy was on finding better ways to link the work of scientists with the needs of society, creating "productive" citizens, and formalizing science as a legitimate school subject. Current calls for science literacy for all have added to this list the importance of literacy in science, whereby literacy includes the deep and thoughtful acquisition of key concepts and ideas, habits of mind, attitudes toward science, and the scientific skills necessary for individuals to be effective members of a technologically and scientifically advanced democratic society.

What is most interesting about the recent call for scientific literacy for all has been its relatively long-lived and widespread support in a larger global context. Although there are vastly different interpretations and implementations of the concept inter- and intranationally, one harmonizing result of this global goal has been the galvanization of a new kind of discourse around what ought to transpire in science classrooms and how that goal might be best attained.

Indeed, proponents of these initiatives view scientific literacy as the educational solution to four concerns: low levels of scientific knowledge; a lack of preparation for using scientific knowledge to make decisions; continued underrepresentation of women and minorities in the sciences; and inadequate science practices in schools (Eisenhart, Finkel, & Marion, 1996). Because of its egalitarian stance, the science for all reform efforts have been seen by science education researchers as crucial to bringing about equity. As the U.S. policy initiative Project 2061 proclaims:

> When demographic realities, national needs, and democratic values are taken into account, it becomes clear that the nation can no longer ignore the science education of any student. Race, language, sex, or economic circumstances must no longer be permitted to be factors in determining who does and who does not receive a good education in science, mathematics and technology. (AAAS, 1989, p. 214)

Yet the policy of science for all has been criticized, and we believe rightly so, for continuing to view the needs of high-poverty, urban youth, non-English-language-background youth, minority students, and girls through the deficit model (Lee & Fradd, 1998; Rodriguez, 1997). The deficit model emerges in science for all in three distinct ways.[2] First, it is assumed that students who come to school not versed in the culture of Western science are "lacking" and need to engage in extra efforts to catch up to their peers. Second, it is assumed that students will prioritize Western ways of knowing, without the backdrop of a culturally situated nature of science. If students do not accept or model these Western values, it is assumed that they are at fault, *not* the instruction or the content of instruction. Third, it is assumed that schools operate meritocratically, that science achievement scores are based on one's efforts and abilities rather than one's degree of enculturation into a system. As Kyle (2001) notes, "The rhetoric of 'science education for all' is juxtaposed to the reality of 'science education for the privileged'" (p. xi). Specifically, for teachers and researchers in high-poverty, urban settings, the science for all campaign fails to provide a useful paradigm for understanding the science education needs and experiences of youth living in urban poverty. Indeed, the designers of Project 2061, a national science education reform initiative in the United States, mentioned previously, state that "teachers should . . . make it clear to female and minority students that they are expected to study the same subjects at the same level as everyone else and to perform as well" (AAAS, 1989, p. 151). This message implies that minority students and females need to work and act like their White male counterparts, not that either science or instruction will be modified to accommodate them. Although it can be argued that this is a call for teachers to engage all students, not just the

White middle-class males, in the academic rigors of science, it can also be read as a call for teachers to encourage acculturation. In the very effort to create inclusive science education communities, the politics of assimilation within schools have become the guide for policy, practice, and curricula.

Reconceptualizing the Deficit Model

Despite this critique, we agree with many researchers in science education that science for all is both a moral and ethical imperative. The current system must be revamped to better reach high-poverty, urban children. Our disagreements rest in how the issues get framed and the import this has for how we understand youth lives and how a practice of science might authentically emerge from them. What would it mean to refocus this review of what we know or need to know about urban youth? How could we thus better understand the issues that divide their science education experiences from those of their more affluent, suburban counterparts? How could we draw away from the deficit model and toward models that are epistemologically consistent with the cultures and worldview of those youth in the inner-city with whom we work (Bernal, 1998)? Indeed, this kind of critical approach to examining the issues that mark the science education experiences of inner-city youth would look quite different because the questions and assumptions that guide such an effort would also look quite different. Although the literature in urban science education is extremely helpful in articulating the issues that divide, we believe that this approach must be tempered with a more holistic understanding of youth's lives in order to help us move beyond a deficit understanding of youth's participation and achievement in science. So in addition to comparing urban youth's academic achievement and access to resources or educative opportunities with those of their more affluent more suburban counterparts, it is important to tease out the answers to the following question: (a) What assumptions about youth lives and the purposes and goals of schooling and school science are embedded in these traditional comparisons? and (b) What might be a more positive, empowering, and epistemologically consistent way of understanding youth lives around these same issues?

A Critical Approach. Before answering these two questions, we will outline in rather broad strokes what we mean by a "critical approach" to science education and why this is important in urban education. We use the phrase *critical approach* to suggest a blending of critical and feminist theories that recognizes that education is "fundamentally concerned with understanding the relationship between power and knowledge" (McLaren, 1989, p. 183). Our perspective rests on the following three major understandings:

First, our understanding of knowledge is grounded in a social constructivist epistemology, which assumes that an individual's or group's knowledge of the world is always subjective and contextually mediated (i.e., constructed within a particular social, political, cultural, economic, historical, and linguistic reality) (Eisenhart et al., 1996; Vygotsky, 1978).

Second, our understanding of power is grounded in the critical traditions' recognition of the explicitly political nature of education, in which it is argued that schooling "must be fundamentally tied to a struggle for a qualitatively better life for all through the construction of a society based on nonexploitative relations and social justice" (McLaren, 1989, p. 172; Nieto, 1999). Viewing the sciences from a critical, social constructivist standpoint leads to a refutation of the positivist myth that there is an objective, solitary way of doing science that results in independent, unbiased knowledge; there is, instead, the implication that the "universalist ideal of a disinterested, detached, objective observer who is free from the limitations of a standpoint . . . has led to a dangerous arrogance regarding the status of scientific knowledge" in Western society (Stanley & Brickhouse, 1995, p. 392). One result of this "dangerous arrogance" is the marginalization, even the destruction, of knowledge systems and ways of knowing that are considered to be inferior within Western science standards (Kyle, 1999; Stanley & Brickhouse, 1995, 2001).

Third, we understand schools as social institutions that are generally focused on more than achievement in learning academic subject matter. Rather, the goals of schooling often center on students learning obedience and how to comply with cultural norms and expectations, especially in high-poverty, urban settings (Oakes, 1990; Page, 1990). For example, success in science class is often more about being good at doing school (i.e., knowing the rules for participation and the expectations of a "good student"), than at doing science (i.e., gaining a deep, conceptual understanding of and an ability to use and produce the science under study) (Lave & Wenger, 1991). Furthermore, the cultural norms, expectations, and rules for participation that are—explicitly and implicitly—brought to the fore and valued in education reflect the social, cultural, economic, and political reality of the culture of power, to the exclusion (or at least the marginalization) of other possible realities.

In short, the critical perspective from which we come challenges assumptions about the purposes and goals of schooling (Freire, 1971; McLaren, 1989); the purpose of an education in the sciences (Brickhouse, 1994; Kyle, 1999, 2001); how science is situated within society, and as a subject in schools (Calabrese Barton, 1998); the traditional roles of teachers and students (Ayers, 1996; Brickhouse & Pottler, 2001; Nieto, 1999, Osborne, 1998); what science is taught, and how (Aikenhead, 1997;

Rodriguez, 1998, 2001); and what science is or should be for, and who can or should do science (Calabrese Barton & Darkside, 2000; Costa, 1995). In summary, critical perspectives offer a foundation for challenging the traditionally held assumptions underlying science education. Indeed, the very belief that students and teachers co-construct knowledge within a politics of location and identity suggests that knowing—knowing science, knowing education, knowing ourselves, knowing others—is historically and politically contextual, and also changeable.

So how does a critical approach to science education reframe our understandings of the literature around urban youth and achievement, resources, and educative opportunities (see Table 2.1)?

Achievement. In terms of academic achievement, instead of narrowly framing youth's successes in science through high-stakes exams, grades, course-taking patterns, or retention and graduation, it is important to consider the kinds of things youth do in out-of-school contexts such as organized clubs

Table 2.1. Reconceptualizing Achievement, Resources, and Opportunity

	Deficit Model: What Students Lack	*Reconceptualized: What Students Bring*
Achievement	High-poverty urban youth lag behind middle-income youth in test scores, high school graduation rates, and school grades	Understanding youth's successes in organized clubs and programs in school, home, and community, while remembering the academic challenges faced by youth in poverty and how these play out in school settings
Resources	High-poverty urban youth attend schools that lack adequate books, lab supplies, and certified teachers	Understanding the human and social capital that are powerful in youth's lives, while remembering the inequities that high-poverty youth experience
Opportunity	High-poverty urban youth lack opportunities to experience challenging curriculum and instructional practices and do high-level coursework (i.e., the pedagogy of poverty)	Understanding what it might mean to begin instruction, class, and school design with students' experiences, resources, and interests in mind, while remaining critical of the "pedagogy of poverty" that is often found in urban schools

or programs or the home or peer-group settings (Fusco, 2001; Rahm, 2002). What would it mean to include in these measures of success how youth might be using science to improve their community or to help raise a family or to care for friends, as Kobe had with the garden project or with his younger siblings? It is also important to consider other ways of making sense of school-based participation (Odegaard & Kyle, 2000; Seiler, 2001). Studies, such as Seiler's (2001), that look at such programs as "lunchtime science," provide us with other accounts of school science achievement. More generally, many of the alternative assessments, such as portfolios and projects (Krajcik, Czerniak, & Berger, 1999), provide other glimpses into what youth's accomplishments in schools might look like. However, many districts and states have moved away from such alternative assessments because they are too subjective, take too long to grade, or are not norm referenced. Further, in many places where these alternative assessments are used, they are graded against a more standard rubric of what constitutes achievement in science, and thus the broader aspects of achievement embedded in such alternative formats are silenced (Fusco, 2001).

What would it mean to broaden our vision of achievement by considering not only what we think youth need to know and be able to do but also what youth believe they might contribute to school science? Kobe, without acknowledging that he had missed *months* of school science, described his teacher as dismissing his attempts to return to science class. Yet Kobe was returning because he actually wanted to have the option of having science as a backup career and because he wanted to share with his peers in his class through the video product he helped to create, what other ways of doing science might look like. This was an immensely risky step for Kobe, for if his teacher had welcomed him back, Kobe, a leading gang member and one who was outwardly proud of being bored at school, would have been willing to share the video. Indeed, Kobe was willing to share a part of his identity rarely seen in school.

Feminist studies of women scientists (Eisenhart & Finkel, 1999) and sociological studies of urban youth centers (McLaughlin, Irby, & Langman, 1994) also provide precedents for this shift in understanding achievement. Eisenhart and Finkel show, through their stories of the work of women scientists, how women are often engaged in science at the margins: an innovative high school genetics class, a school-to-work internship for prospective engineers, environmental action groups, and nonprofit conservation agencies. These places, not often thought of first as "places of science" but rather as places that involve science intensively, are populated with high proportions of women who are succeeding in and enjoying their work. Eisenhart and Finkel also show how many of these women personally measure their success with qualities that are not part of the traditional success scale. Instead of gauging their success in terms of numbers of publications or amounts of grant dollars, many of the women in their study spoke about the positive impact of their work on the lives of others or on the environment, how well they taught and collaborated with others in their labs, and even how much time they were able to spend away from the lab with people who were important in their lives (children, parents, significant others). The authors' claim is not that these are "female" qualities that must be considered or that traditional qualities had no bearing on these women's professional advancement. Rather, their claim is that the women whom they studied, as a group, held broader visions of success in science. In a parallel but more implicit fashion, McLaughlin and colleagues (1994) describe the nature and quality of those urban spaces, or "urban sanctuaries," where high-poverty, minority, urban youth thrive. The authors make claims about what it is that is important to youth about these places and how youth then construct their lives and identities through such places. These descriptions, too, grow out of a much broader vision of what it means to succeed in society. They focus on qualities such as responsiveness to youth concerns, youth authority in program development, and the importance of sustaining relationships. Thus, it seems that these studies, and studies like them (see in particular, Fusco, 2001; Nieto, 1999; Valenzuela, 1999), give us ways to think about achievement that are more positive, empowering, and consistent with the lives of urban youth.

Resources. Like achievement, the issue of resources can be reexamined. The literature on resources tends to revolve around the kinds of physical capital that is missing (or at best, inadequately present) in the lives of youth who experience urban poverty, including such things as school-based materials, home/community-based materials, and school-based and extramural programs. This crucial area of study should not be overlooked. Poverty, by its nature, sets up an economic barrier that makes access to a multitude of resources difficult. However, we argue, it is also important to consider the kinds of resources to which children and youth in urban poverty already have access; how those resources get framed, sometimes in very negative ways, by those in power positions; and how they might be reframed in productive and powerful ways.

While nearly everyone in the science education community would certainly agree that all children need equitable access to resources, resources are often defined in narrow terms, as instructional texts or classroom materials (National Science Teachers Association [NSTA], 1998). When we consider access to resources as a requirement for inclusion, the very definition of *resources* must be broadened. Kobe's story provides some insight here. Embedded in it are glimpses of the kinds of human and social capital that are powerful in his life (Spillane, Diamond, Walker, Havelson, & Jita, 2001). While involved in the lot project, Kobe helped the other youth think through the challenges they would face (from competing groups of youngsters) in keeping the lot safe and clean. He also brought his understanding of his younger sibling's play needs to broadening the conversation around the kinds of things that might be added to the community lot. He created nontraditional ways to become involved in the garden project through conducting interviews and producing a video documentary. Kobe's relationships with and leadership of his peers as a gang leader influenced how many youth ultimately participated in the video documentary and helped frame the documentary as something that was cool and youth centered rather than something that was too academic, too White, or too university centered. Thus, a student's individual knowledge, skills, and expertise and his or her relations among his or her peers and family (including younger siblings) are important resources that ought to be included in the science education curriculum.

One of the issues here is that because of the ways in which science education and schooling have been constructed historically, these very kinds of resources have not been viewed as important or something that will make a significant difference in youth's development in science. After all, Kobe's parenting skills have little connection to the advanced placement (AP) science curriculum, and his gang involvement often bordered on criminal activity. Yet there is precedent for thinking about resources more broadly, and the ways in which one values what youth and their families bring to school can change the practice of schooling.

Delgado-Gaitan's (1996) work with immigrant families in California provides a particularly thoughtful framework. She describes how parent and teacher attitudes, school programs, and organizational structures changed in one school district when the kinds of human and social resources that immigrant parents brought to school (including language and home- and community-based practices, activities, and celebrations) were acknowledged publicly within the school setting. In science education, Spillane and colleagues (2001), in describing how a small set of Chicago schools that serve low-income populations confronted the issue of resources, demonstrate how the very practice of school science can be transformed for the better when individuals work together to mobilize physical, human, and social capital. Tobin, Roth, and Zimmermann (2001) describe similar approaches to utilizing capital in the process of learning to teach in high-poverty, urban high schools. These studies are important because

that science ought to look like. Although this understanding of students' learning in science is indeed helpful, it does not get us far enough, especially when we are working with populations whose uses for and production of science might be vastly different from our own or from those documented and described in policy initiatives and national frameworks (Rodriguez, 1997).

In our own work with urban youth who are living in circumstances of economic hardship, we have felt that each and every time that we have tried to make sense of why youth do what they do in science-related experiences through analyzing what science they know, what habits of mind they bring to the process, or what skills or behaviors they engage in, our understandings of these youth and their lives have fallen short. We may have been able to determine what concepts the youth learned—or failed to learn—by participating in any given activity, but we did not really have a clear understanding of why some activities failed while others succeeded in ways that we, as the teachers or researchers, could never have dreamed could do so on our own.

For example, in reflecting on Kobe's experiences with school, we knew that his resistance to what went on in his 9th- and 10th-grade science classes was influenced by a very complex set of circumstances. Kobe believed that his teachers did not care for him, that science was boring and had nothing to do with his career aspirations, and that he needed to act tough with his teachers to demonstrate his autonomy. Kobe had family- and peer-related responsibilities outside school that would have been daunting for any teenager. These out-of-school responsibilities, because of their immediacy, quite frequently took priority over schooling, which only seemed to emphasize long-term goals, making success in school science just that much more difficult. Although Kobe, over time, became successful in the after-school science program, even at the height of his participation he was still often viewed as peripheral to the after-school science project.

Contemporary understandings of scientific literacy for all help us to understand what Kobe learned in school science and in after-school science, but they do not help us to understand how or why Kobe activated those skills or knowledge within and across those two domains of community and school. We get a sense of how well the science that Kobe learned matches up to the ideal scientifically literate person, but we do not gain a better sense of how or why his own values and life contexts were important to his development or decisions to pursue science. We may be able to describe the habits of mind that Kobe brought to bear in out-of-school science and why those values failed him in school science, but we do not understand how those habits of mind have been framed by the social, cultural, and political discourses that characterize schooling, his family life, or his peer groups. Finally, we may be able to understand Kobe as an individual learner, but we do not get a sense of how Kobe's participation, in both productive and destructive ways, is supported by his location within a community of people and a network of resources (whatever or whoever they may be). Gaining a sense of why Kobe did what he did—either in his rejection of school science and his later fleeting embrace of school science, or in his gradual increased participation in after-school science and what we thought he learned there—requires us to understand how Kobe's science achievements are much broader than what science he learned. His engagement in science involved making sense of how and why he engaged (or did not engage) in science in the different domains of his life and how his engagement changed with changing contexts, peer relations, experiences, and time. I (Angie) was excited to witness Kobe's return to school so that he could have science as a backup career, and disappointed to learn that even though his own understandings of science (and himself in science) changed, his new strategies for engaging in science were not recognized in school.

A Practice of Science

The phrase *a practice of science* is meant to convey what people *do* with and in science, or in other words, how people understand, use, and produce science in the different domains that make up their lives.

A practice of science among youth (or anyone else for that matter) is shaped in three ways: events, structures, and identities (see Figure 2.1).

Science Events. There are the actual *science events* that youth have opportunities to participate in (or help to create). In literacy studies, Heath (1982) has defined a literacy event as "any occasion in which a piece of writing is integral to the nature of the participants' interactions and their interpretive processes" (p. 93). Hamilton (2000) has furthered this definition to include the concept that events are local activities, influenced by local context and culture. As Hamilton did for literary events in literacy studies, we have taken a rather liberal definition of science events to cast a broad net. We count events that one might traditionally label as scientific, such as school science labs, after-school science projects, or home-based experimentation. We also count those events that are science related, and described as such by either the youth in our study or by us, such as making videos about science and life in the inner city, discussions about child care and health issues, or playing computer games (see also Heath, 1999).

When we look at science events, we are interested in the parameters of the event: in who participates in these events, what activities actually

different domains to generate a list of practices that appeared to be important to a particular child or to a particular domain (see Table 2.2). In examining specific domains, we paid careful attention to the social structures
that influenced the events we were examining, including their spoken and
unspoken rules, the social and material capital available and activated, and
the modes of and opportunities for participation. For example, if the event
under investigation transpired in school, then we reflected upon what rules,
both formal and informal, shaped such things as participation, discursive
practices, relationships, and resources. Third, we compared practices across
specific youth and across domains.

LOOKING AHEAD

As we have looked closely at the events, structures, and relationships that
frame our work with the youth in our studies, four major themes have
emerged that help us to describe youth's practices of science:

- Power and co-opting science spaces
- Relevant science: Activating resources in nonstandard ways
- Transformations: Science as a tool for change
- Community

As we described earlier, the phrase *a practice of science* is meant to convey what people *do* with and in science, or in other words, how people
understand, use, and produce science in the different domains that make
up their lives. Thus, as we will show in the following chapters, each of these
themes is important in two distinct ways. First, each theme reflects an
overarching desire or goal expressed by youth in their efforts to understand
the role and importance of science in their lives—*what science is and why
they do it*. Second, each theme reflects how the youth choose to participate
in science (the kinds of actions in which youth engage, and when and how
they engage in those actions), and the meaning they bring to those actions
(the beliefs they draw upon, and the ideals they value to sustain their engagement). Each theme is not a "practice" in and of itself, but rather describes the terrain that allows their science practices to grow and thrive.

In the following five chapters (Chapters 3–7) we separately examine
each one of the themes listed earlier. In examining each theme, we set up
our discussion in the following manner:

- We provide an explanation of how we define the key ideas that make
  up the theme; we describe how the theme connects to and departs

Table 2.2. A Framework for Making Sense of Youth's Science Events and Practices

	Analyzing Youth's Practices Across Events in the Same Domain			
Understanding a Science Event	Identity: Relationships, Personal Experience	Activities: Actions, Knowledge and Skills, Attitudes	Structures: Space and Capital	Examining Practices Across Domains
What is the social nature of science events? What do youth know and learn about science (knowledge, habits of mind, and attitudes)? What are the event parameters (activities, participants, setting, and artifacts)?	What kinds of relationships are shaped by or informed by the science events? between whom? for what purposes? What/when/how do youth make judgments about their worlds in relation to the science events? How do they relate these judgments to the science in the event and to the nonscience in the event?	What attitudes and values do the participants express in the science events? What actions do the participants actually engage in, and what are their stated motivations for doing so? How do youth talk about what the science in the event is and why it is (or isn't) important in their lives or to their community? Which actions are youth most conscious of? What skills and knowledge do youth need to know to engage in different practices, and where do they get this knowledge?	How are the science events connected to (or disconnected from) the context, their culture, and their neighborhood? What resources do youth draw upon? How do they activate these resources?	What science practices do youth engage in in different contexts, in particular, classroom science, after-school science, in the neighborhood with peer groups, and at home? How do these practices differ? What can these differences tell us in terms of different forms/ kinds of scientific literacy? the value of science in youth's lives? the reasons why youth engage in science in different contexts/ domains? How we might better draw upon youth's lives in school-based settings?

44

JUAN: Because those are science. Making things isn't science.
It's like building things. Construction.
TANAHIA: Building things is like what?
JUAN: Like construction.
TANAHIA: Juan, can you tell me if you've ever done anything like this at school?
JUAN: Um, no.
TANAHIA: Why do you think you have not?
JUAN: Um, I guess because we don't do that in school.

INTRODUCTION: WORLDS APART

In the first of these quotes, Darkside and Goldberg, both 10th graders from Southside Shelter, discuss their lack of opportunities for learning science in their school. Unlike most of their peers who attend the nearby large comprehensive high school, both attend a medium-sized high school that has a focus on leadership and justice. Their school prides itself on its high academic standards and its success in serving a highly diverse but also overwhelmingly high-poverty population. The school, which provides free lunch to more than 90% of its student body, sends almost one fourth of its students on to 4-year colleges, a statistic that, although much higher than that of neighboring public schools, is much lower than the city average of 51%. A quick look at the official school statistics shows that even though 30% of the student population is overage at the time they enter the 9th grade, the school itself boasts a 76% graduation rate within 4 academic years. A conversation with the principal of the school reveals that she is proud of the college preparatory nature of the curriculum her school offers and the caliber of her teaching staff. She sees her school as a haven far different from the larger comprehensive high schools—her students have a chance to learn to act and think for themselves and to be supported in trying out academic identities.

Goldberg and Darkside's conversation provides us with a glimpse into how students understand life in school. Goldberg senses that his school life is marginal to what other youth his age might have—he does not believe he has access to science in all 4 years of high school and feels that when he does enroll in science courses his teachers "don't explain nothing." Darkside, however, is far more critical than Goldberg. He uses his understanding of his life in the margins, as he says, "to set Goldberg straight." He knows science is offered in all 4 years, but he also knows that not all students get science or even get the choice to select science. He believes

that most students do not really know that they can enroll in science because they believe what they are told, even when it is not true. Although
he is less critical of Goldberg in how science gets taught, he chalks up his
lack of criticism to opportunity. It seems that Darkside is willing to do what
he needs to do to succeed in poorly taught classes, so long as he has the
chance to take them.

If we look at the conversation with Juan, a student living at Hope
Shelter, we see the same kind of conflict. Juan's teachers shared with us
that his school struggles with student achievement, and that they are on
the verge of being labeled a "failing" school—a label given to the lowest
achieving schools in the district. Consequently, the teachers at his elementary school concentrate on improving student achievement in math and
reading so that students may perform adequately on the states' high-stakes
assessment. Students who "do not engage" in classroom learning are sent
to BMC (behavior modification counseling) so that they do not disrupt other
children's learning, and so that they do not lose valuable instructional time
themselves. According to one of the teachers, BMC is basically an "in-school
suspension program" that takes disruptive students out of class and places
them under direct adult guidance whereby they are given quiet opportunities to practice their math and reading skills with worksheets and other
individual activities. Juan interprets this situation as about attending a
school where teachers are mean because they do not care about students
and do not teach anything but math and reading.

How could the worlds of schooling look so different for youth from
how they appear to the leaders of their schools? In each of these short
quotes, the youth, all homeless, have an astonishing awareness of how
different their school experiences are from what they could be. From their
experiences in school science and those in Hope and Southside Shelters,
these young people are well aware of how social institutions rely on
human, social, and material resources to separate those with and without power. Yet these young people are not without agency. They find
ways to activate the resources to which they have access, whether they
be material resources or social, human, or symbolic resources, to critique
how they have been positioned on the margin and to try to change that
reality for the better. We see this in the way in which Darkside responds
to Goldberg's critique and in his attempts to convince Goldberg that he
does have choices.

In this chapter we explore what it means to live and learn in the margins and how youth learn to use their social positioning to their advantage.
In the previous chapter, we described how current policy initiatives and
research in science education focus on what children in poverty or children of color lack. One of the beliefs that fuels deficit model thinking is

that children living in urban poverty come from social and cultural communities that cannot provide them with valuable resources. This is where the terms *disadvantaged* and *children at risk* come from. An examination of youth lives in the borderland shows us the strength and power that exists in the social and cultural places occupied by children from high-poverty, urban communities. It is in these places that they gain the cultural wisdom, social critique, and political solidarity to stand up to the strong assimilation forces of schools, science, and society that lead to the perpetuation of negative myths about their lives. Children living in urban poverty may not always learn standard school knowledge such as standard English or textbook science, but as we will show, they gain a repertoire of strategies of action that can be powerful forces.

LIVING WITHIN THE MARGINS

Margin and center concerns have been noteworthy in the science education reform discourse. As described in Chapter 2, science education reform has been guided by the slogan "science for all." Feminist and multicultural science educators have elevated the significance of the science-for-all discourse by pushing the science education community to consider questions such as, Whose values, beliefs, and experiences have been a part of science historically, and whose have not? Who participates in science and who does not? How do teachers ensure that all of their students' ideas, experiences, ways of knowing, and community are valued in the classroom science community? The main conclusion accepted by feminists and multicultural science educators is that if science could be taught in ways that encouraged a broader vision of science, the margin-center dichotomy could be collapsed in science class, suggesting at some level that all students would be granted adequate access to effective learning opportunities in science.

However, at least for the population of homeless children about whom we write, the margin-center dichotomy has not been collapsed so easily. There are many issues besides access to science or good science teaching that feed into the dichotomy.

This dichotomy fundamentally implies separation, and at its nucleus is the issue of resources. It is what individuals and communities have access to and how those resources are valued that set them apart. What individuals and communities have access to and can activate, however, is not just based on material resources, such as books or supplies or even money.

As described in the previous chapter, resources include human, social, and symbolic resources in addition to material resources. Thus, the margin and center also denote different social spaces, with their own as-

sociated structures that foster their own cultural, social, and political boundaries; cultural toolkits; and social relations. Although these boundaries are
themselves weak and in a constant state of flux, they are used by those with
greater social and material power to demonstrate differentness, usually in
a hierarchical way. So, for example, if we return to the quotes that opened
this chapter, we can see how Darkside and Goldberg are positioned on the
margins because of the kinds of resources they have access to and can activate. They are economically impoverished and attend a high school that
is limited in resources. Goldberg is unaware of his right to attend a science
class and shrugs it off, attributing this situation to scheduling.

However, critical feminist studies have taken the margin and center
analysis further to show that the margin can also serve as a powerful so-
cializing setting for oppressed people, a place where they can learn to deal
with the individual and institutional racism and other prejudice that is
prevalent in society, and to develop empowering attitudes toward their
own ethnicity that may not be as visibly active as the prevailing negative
images and evaluations of oppressed groups in popular culture (Ward,
2000). In fact, Chicana feminists have adopted the term *borderland* instead
of *the margin* to acknowledge the powerful, critical, political stance supported by and sustained through a shared history of domination and resistance (Anzaldúa, 1987; Bernal, 1998; Elenes, 2001).

Perhaps the most important quality of the borderland or the margin
lies in how it supports solidarity building through shared access and activation of resources that are not valued in other social settings. In the borderland, solidarity building happens through sharing resources or strategies
of action and through challenging dominant thinking patterns. For example,
if youth learn to place cultural knowledge on equal footing with academic
knowledge, they can learn to situate official school knowledge as a cultural
practice and to debunk the deficit model for its definitions of school success and failure.

In Chapter 2 we discussed how, at the core of the youth's practice of
science are events, structures, and identities. Each of these domains, and
how they intersect with resources, plays a hand in how youth are positioned in the margin and center, and in their authority to name their own
science practices. When the margin-center dichotomy is only understood
through physical circumstances and institutionalized rules, it is treated
as if it were fixed and changeable only through rectifying deficits. If the
margin and center are viewed as social and political settings informed
by cultures, experiences, and histories, there is a way to see how youth
can use the margin in their identity and relationship building and in their
participation in science events to create new worlds of importance and
power.

MARGIN-CENTER SEPARATION:
CLAUDIA'S AND JUAN'S STORIES

Understanding the power of the borderland for those who have been viewed as marginal in schools or society provides a framework for understanding the challenges that high-poverty, urban youth face in learning science and how they choose to respond to those challenges.

In what follows, we present short portraits of two of the young people: Claudia and Juan. We selected these two youth because their lives reflect different interests, directions, and responses to schooling and to life in the margin. After we present the two portraits, we look across these youth's stories to make sense of how they use the margin or the borderland as a place of separation, strength, growth, and solidarity building. We use these stories to foreshadow youths' practices of science presented in forthcoming chapters and how these practices emerge from the strengths of the borderland.

CLAUDIA

We first met Claudia when she was in fourth grade and lived in supportive housing at Hope Shelter. Through conversation we learned that she was born and had lived for the first 3 years of her life in one of the neighboring Mexican states, after which her family immigrated to Texas, where she has lived since. When Claudia was 6, she moved to a local short-term homeless shelter with her mother and two brothers to escape domestic violence. Claudia's mother attributed the family violence to the stresses of living in a new land with few resources and to differing priorities between her husband and herself for the distribution of what little resources they had, especially as it related to her children's opportunities. Claudia's mother was a strong woman who resisted traditional channels of authority in order to create opportunities for her children. Although she believed that leaving her husband was the best decision for her children, she talked about feeling ashamed of leaving him and of moving to a shelter. When Claudia's family's time in the short-term shelter expired, they were granted space in Hope Shelter, having met three key criteria: the family income was below the poverty level; they did not have immediate family in the area; and Claudia's mother was actively seeking better paying employment.

Although all the children and their families at the shelter were living under conditions of economic hardship, Claudia's situation appeared to be particularly distressed. Our visits to her shelter home nearly always revealed an empty refrigerator and empty shelves, and only a few pieces of furniture that were somewhat run down. The shelter provided furniture for families in need, but Claudia's family appeared to possess the bare minimum. We found Claudia's behavior around her peers and us to be framed by these conditions, which marked her as being different from her peers at the shelter. We remember one afternoon at the start of Science Club, when we were having an impromptu series of running races in the area behind the shelter and checking our heartbeats and respiration at the start and finish of each race. One of the boys, Juan, had an ice cream cone that he had brought from home before the start of Science Club. While he was eating it, the ice cream fell off the cone and onto the ground. Some of the children laughed at Juan, but he just shrugged it off. He was about to throw the remainder of his cone on the ground when Claudia asked Juan for the cone, picked the ice cream up off the ground, wiped off the dirt, and proceeded to eat the rest of the ice cream. Some of the students laughed at Claudia because eating ice cream that fell on the ground was "nasty." Claudia gave those children mean looks and continued to eat her ice cream.

Our observations of and interactions with Claudia in Science Club revealed to us that she was creative, resourceful, bright, and energetic. Not only was she fluent in English and Spanish, but she also moved easily back and forth between languages as situations dictated. In fact, we noticed that she was often kept home from school to translate for her mother. We also found Claudia to be a mentally and physically strong girl. On several occasions, we witnessed her becoming the brunt of boys' jokes. Many boys attempted to pick on her because her beautiful, large, round eyes reminded them of the eyes of a frog. They called her *el sapo* (the toad) bringing her close to tears. We also observed these same boys pulling at her clothes and throwing paper at her as she walked home from the bus stop. Claudia did not take this harassment lightly. She always fought back. On several occasions we witnessed her instigating physical fights with some of the boys to prove her status and strength. Although she was small, she was strong, quick, and aggressive. Many other girls who lived at the shelter looked up to Claudia because of these qualities. However, by the same token, she was somewhat alienated from the cliques of the more traditionally feminine girls.

Claudia: Why I Don't Like Science

Perhaps even more than her willful spirit in dealing with the boys, what really distinguished Claudia for us was how this spirit manifested itself in her relationship to schooling. Claudia received tremendous amounts of homework from her teachers. Quite often, we found her in the portable, copying all her times tables, 1 through 10, writing out lists of 100 words that began with the letter *a, b, c,* and so on and completing multipage worksheets of basic skills math problems. Even when other youth were building kites or playing tag, she often resisted the games to work on her assigned homework. Claudia had a clear desire to succeed in school. However, her report card indicated the opposite: She was barely making average grades. She also spoke passionately about how much she "hated" school. In fact, she admitted to us on more than one occasion that she did not talk very much in school and did not raise her hand in class, because she wanted her teacher to know she was bored:

> I never like school, mostly because it's boring. It's boring because we have teachers and work, and we never play. I always have to be here, be there, do this, do that, and I am always getting in trouble. It's not even my fault, and I get in trouble. If schools did not have teachers, then it might be fun. . . . You know why I don't raise my hand in school? Because I want my teacher to know I'm bored!

Claudia saw the kinds of work she was asked to do in school as "boring" and "stupid," and she wished she had more opportunities to work on things that interested her.

On the one hand, Claudia's failure to thrive in school didn't surprise us. She attended a resource-strapped school that was under fire for its low test scores and that provided the teachers with a "poverty sensitivity training" program that we believed to be discriminatory. On the other hand, despite these stories, Claudia desired to excel in school, and she worked hard during after-school hours to complete her homework.

Claudia, though she seemed to enjoy the activities presented in Science Club, was particularly vocal about not liking school science. In fact, of all of the school subjects, she claimed that science was one of her worst. Math and reading were her favorite subjects. We often wondered if this was the case because in her school—noted for low state test scores in math and reading—there was an inordinate emphasis on test preparation in math and reading. When science was taught, it often involved basic reading activities and few hands-on opportunities to experiment or play with the world around her. As she says of science: "I don't like science. It is boring. All we do is read." Claudia was insistent that the reason why she did not do well was not that she wasn't smart enough. Claudia, in fact, had a strong sense of self and a powerful sense of her capabilities. She felt that her low grades were a result of the fact that science class was boring, and she never had the chance to get "used to science."

Claudia was also quick to call her teacher mean, and by this she meant several different things: Teachers were mean if they did not listen, did not do fun activities in the classroom, or were too strict. Underlying each of these definitions of being mean was Claudia's deeply held desire to feel respected—to be listened to and cared for.

Doing Science and Activating Resources

Despite Claudia's description of not liking science in school and being bored by it, she did have opportunities to engage in different kinds of science activities in and out of school. Sometimes these drew upon resources that were part of her cultural toolkit and appeared to pull her into science learning and open up new science worlds to her. Other times these experiences seemed to demand something that she was not adequately prepared to give, and separated her even further from success in science. We share three stories to make this point: Writing Reports, Shoebox Camera, and The Desk.

Writing Reports. Claudia reported that her favorite school science activity involved a study in which she and her classmates were engaged whose theme was "plants today." She was particularly interested in where plants grow and what they need to survive. The activity that she enjoyed so much was composed of two parts: reading two pages about plants and, following that, writing a report to be shared with the class. Claudia stated that she enjoyed this activity because she "liked writing reports." She was a good writer, and making up stories was always "fun" for her. Claudia's enjoyment of this activity was interesting to us because it involved the very kind of science activities she claimed to find boring. However, when the reading was coupled with writing, an area of strength she enjoyed, her ideas about science changed. Writing reports as a favored experience was also supported by Claudia's ideas for what to include in a student-made video about "what science teachers should know about kids." Claudia worked hard to persuade the three other girls involved in making the video that part of it should be focused on describing different science activities that could involve report writing. In the video project she included examples of report writing about plants, rocks, and spaceships.

The Shoebox Camera. The second story is about Claudia's experiences in school science that involved making a shoebox camera, a project about which she was initially excited because she could keep the camera and the camera would work. To build the shoebox camera, Claudia's teacher requested that each student bring in his or her own shoebox. For those students who did not have shoeboxes at home, the teacher provided a list of shoestores that would give students free shoeboxes. She also allowed them to purchase boxes from her for 50¢. Her reason for charging 50¢ was that she wanted to instill in the students a responsibility for their own education. This request frustrated Claudia because she did not have a shoebox at home. She reported that her mother could not take her to the store because her family did not own a car, nor could her mother speak English. She also did not have 50¢ to spend on a shoebox and said that if she did, she wouldn't waste it on a shoebox!

When Claudia brought neither a shoebox nor money to school, her teacher offered her the opportunity to clean the erasers during recess to earn the shoebox. Claudia chose not to clean the erasers, because she was "mad" at her teacher, but when science class came around that afternoon, her teacher gave her a shoebox anyway. Claudia thought that the shoebox was ugly and poked holes in her box (rather than make the camera correctly) because she did not want to make a camera anymore. She was eventually reprimanded by her teacher for poking the holes, and in the end felt as if their teacher did not care about her and that science, no matter what she did, was boring.

Claudia's Desk. Claudia stood with her hands on both hips, looking proudly at the desk in front of her. Even a brief glance in her direction provoked from her the immediate response "This desk is mine!" along with a determined look on her face that seemed to suggest that she meant business. The desk was small but functional. It contained no drawers, but furnished a writing surface large enough for any young person and stood sturdily upon the floor. The desk, or rather, "Claudia's desk," as it became affectionately known among the youth and teachers at Hope Shelter, was crafted carefully from six pieces of wood and with many, many nails. In the end, the desk stood two and a half feet tall, two and half feet wide and two feet deep. However simple, the desk was a testament to Claudia's generative capacities. Indeed, during a single afternoon, Claudia, a lively fourth grader, conceptualized, designed, and built her desk with only limited adult help.

Claudia's desk building was not a part of the plan for after-school science at Hope Shelter that day. Rather, the plan was to continue with the butterfly garden project by building above-ground planters. For the 6 weeks prior to this episode, the youth had been caring for caterpillars. We had begun this project for several reasons: The youth in the after-school program had expressed an ongoing interest in having pets, and they constantly used after-school science as a legitimate way to bring living creatures into the shelter community, where such things were normally prohibited. Caring for caterpillars captured this interest among the students. There were other reasons why we selected this particular project: Monarch butterflies are the state insect of Texas, and Texas is a primary resting point on their migration route between their northern summer homes and their southern winter destinations of Mexico and South America. Further, butterflies are a rich part of Mexican and Indigenous American culture. For example, among some tribes of Mexico, the butterfly is a symbol of the fertility of the earth, and in pre-Hispanic Mexican Indian culture, the butterfly is one of the symbolic representatives of the god of rain. Finally, ecological interactions, migration, and life cycles are key concepts in science and would help us pull together our ongoing efforts to understand the local neighborhood scientifically.

Because Hope Shelter planned on the future construction of new housing, we were prevented from planting the butterfly garden in the ground near the portable building that housed the after-school program. Instead, we would have to use several small above-ground planters, so that we could move the garden to another location if necessary. The youth conducted research on butterflies and their habitats and then designed their gardens through blueprints, pictures, and supply lists and much debate over what was really needed. On the day we brought in the agreed-upon materials, the majority of the youth set about assembling their planters. Claudia, however, who appeared on this particular day to be disinterested in the activity, asked us if she could use some of the wood to build a desk. We asked her if she was sure that that was what she wanted to do. After all, in the preceding weeks she had been very much into taking care of the caterpillars and researching how to best care for the soon-to-be butterflies. She had thoughtfully planned her butterfly garden and had carefully selected the pattern and colors for her flowers in order to best please her fledgling butterfly. Claudia insisted she wanted to build a desk, and so, in not quite knowing how to respond to her, we encouraged her creativity. While the other students built planters, Claudia and Tanahia went inside the portable to work on Claudia's desk.

For Claudia, the six pieces of wood intended to form the sides and bottom of a planter became the sides and top of a desk, a piece of furniture that she wanted for her shelter apartment. She had played our science game as any good student would for as long as she could. She did not explicitly tell us that the planter-building activity did not meet her changing needs that day. However, when presented with the opportunity to act on her needs, her actions clearly demonstrated this fact. As teachers, we had thought that we were being student centered in our teaching decisions about the caterpillars and butterfly garden. However, being student centered is not always the same as encouraging student authorship or ownership. When Claudia's family moved out of the shelter, she took her desk with her. Two other youth, of about the same age as Claudia, who built a planter in the same afternoon that Claudia built her desk, and who moved out of Hope Shelter around the same time as did Claudia's family, did not take their planter with them. Upon their departure, their beautifully decorated planter remained outside the door of their former shelter apartment.

JUAN

When we first met Juan, he was a fifth-grade student and had been living at Hope Shelter for about a year and a half with his mother, brother, and two younger sisters. Juan, of Mexican American heritage, was fluent in both English and Spanish. Although he only spoke Spanish with his mother, we rarely witnessed him speaking Spanish outside the home.

Juan appeared to be a friendly, outgoing early adolescent. He enjoyed playing football, soccer, and baseball and talked about why he liked being with his friends at school: "They're cool and we say funny jokes." We have observed him on many occasions interacting with his peers, trading Pokemon cards, and discussing the WWF (World Wrestling Federation). However, we have also observed a young person who often sat alone and quietly watched other children and events. Because of his sometimes soft-spoken nature and bashful smile, Juan could be mistaken for a person who was much more reserved—at times, almost shy.

Living by the Rules

Juan's descriptions of school can be categorized into two kinds of talk. He spoke positively of school when he talked about his friends or about opportunities to do such things as play sports. His talk almost always turned negative when he discussed academic and behavioral concerns. His grades were always high enough to pass him from grade to grade, but he did not excel in school in any of his classes and did not stand out for any of the counselors or teachers with whom we talked.

Juan infrequently talked about the academic side of school, and when he did so, his comments were shrouded in a sense that he had little control over what happened there. He was quite guarded when discussing his grades and schooling. His school talk almost always wound around descriptions of the unfair consequences of schooling:

> JUAN: [My teacher last year] was mean.
> TANAHIA: Why do you think that she was mean?
> JUAN: She was mean.
> TANAHIA: Can you give me an example?
> JUAN: Um, she sent me to the office too many times.

TANAHIA: Why did she send you to the office?
JUAN: I don't know.
TANAHIA: What were you doing right before she sent you to the
    office?
JUAN: Drawing.
TANAHIA: Drawing, and you were supposed to be doing . . . ?
JUAN: Math.
TANAHIA: Do you think that's a good reason to send someone to
    the office?
JUAN: No.
TANAHIA: What else could she have done?
JUAN: Put me in time out.
TANAHIA: Put you in time out? For how long?
JUAN: Thirty minutes.
TANAHIA: And then after you came out of time out do you think
    that you would have done your math?
JUAN: Yeah.
TANAHIA: What happened when you got sent to the office?
JUAN: I had BMC [behavior modification counseling].
TANAHIA: What's that?
JUAN: Where like . . . you have to stay in a room the whole day.

Responding to rules (and the consequences of breaking them) occupied a great deal of Juan's time. He spoke openly of the community service that he had to perform as a penalty for breaking rules at the shelter or for misbehaving. The impact of BMC, referrals, and community service appeared to be deeply grounded in his life:

TANAHIA: If there were one thing that Hope could change, what
    would you like it to be?
JUAN: No more community service.
(*Later*)
TANAHIA: What's one thing you wish your school would change?
JUAN: No more referrals.
TANAHIA: No more referrals? What are referrals? What do they do?
JUAN: They send me to the office.
TANAHIA: And what happens when they send you to the office?
JUAN: You go to BMC.

Indeed, Juan's description of being sent to the office and of doing community service at the shelter reflected a recurrent theme in most of our interactions with him: his own perceived lack of power to change the norms for participation in institutional settings and its impact on his present and future circumstances. The structures (BMC, referrals) and people (teachers, after-school staff) with power loomed over Juan, sometimes seeming insurmountable to him. His response most often was to resist the rules and to suffer the consequences. The effect that this power structure had on Juan was seen when he was asked what things he would change about Hope Shelter and his school. Without any reservation, he stated, "No more community service" and "No more referrals."

Science in and out of School

Juan had very distinct opinions about what things constituted science. The quote that opened this chapter showed Juan describing the picnic table project and how he did not believe the project to be science. From this excerpt it is evident to us that Juan had clear ideas about what science could be and that these ideas were influenced by traditional curricular practices. For instance, dissecting frogs and snakes are widely acceptable activities in U.S. science classrooms; whereas conducting projects, such as the picnic table project, are typically not part of the school science curriculum.

One poignant illustration of how Juan's black-and-white distinction of what science was occurred while the class was making wooden planters in the after-school science program. In the beginning of the project, all the students sat outside and attempted to assemble their wood. Probably having observed some of the others struggling, Juan left his planter and went over to assist one of the other children. He exclaimed, "Let me do it. I'm good at this." Then, we did not think much about the statement. We simply jotted it down in our field notes and continued to assist some of the other students. Later, as we reflected on some of the conversations in which Juan talked about these building activities as "construction" and not science, we wondered what else he perceived himself as "good at" and if those areas were similarly disconnected from academic subjects (see Figure 3.1).

Through our interviews, we learned that Juan desired to work as a "rocklayer" when he is older:

TANAHIA: (*Referring to the steps followed in making the picnic table*) Do you think that we could use that in our everyday life?

JUAN: Yeah.

TANAHIA: How do you think we can use those skills?

JUAN: Well, every time when I grow bigger and I get better at them and better and better, I can make that into a job.

TANAHIA: And what skills did you learn here that would help you out?

Figure 3.1. Juan and construction.

JUAN: Hammering, drilling, sawing, a lot of things.
TANAHIA: Can you tell me why you want to be a rocklayer, or brick-
    layer?
JUAN: Um, the reason I want to is because I just like it, laying rock.
    And I like being outside so I think that's what I'm going to do.
TANAHIA: How do you think that you could find that kind of job?
    Where would you go? Or, how would you prepare for it?
JUAN: All places. Buy a truck, get some tools, go all over the world.
    Go to Canada, go to China, go everywhere. Go to Houston,
    Dallas.

While some would propose that this description is just the product of
the vivid imagination of a young boy, others might be more critical, stating that Juan's career choice was mediated by the culture in which he had
been immersed. Juan appeared to know the route to becoming a rocklayer.
Jobs in the field of construction are by no means to be looked upon as being
inferior. However, one cannot help but wonder if Juan's decision to work
in construction had been resolved by his assumption that he was not good
at school. In his estimation, it appeared that construction was *separate* from
"school subjects." Furthermore, working "outside" was viewed as separate from a more "academic" career, when in fact there are numerous ca-

reers in science that require extensive amounts of work outdoors. However, this view of science being contained only in a classroom was most likely constructed by the way in which Juan had experienced science instruction both in and out of school. Consequently, had he purposely excluded other jobs in favor of a career that he felt was more promising than what was considered the academic track?

When Juan declared that he would "buy a truck, get some tools, [and] go all over the world," what surfaced in his statement was his desire for autonomy. Juan could be his own boss in construction, and he would be given the freedom to do what he enjoyed doing. It appeared from his statements that Juan, as a fifth grader, had become disenchanted with the idea of school. School was a place where he had little autonomy or power. We thus see his choosing a career in construction as a purposeful act of rebellion (against the traditional academic path to success) and self-preservation (his valuing a set of experiences and an identity not part of school).

However, there were a few occasions when Juan moved against these patterns of self-preservation and of rebellion against academic values in school. For example, he described with great excitement and enthusiasm his participation in a water balloon experiment conducted outdoors. When Juan spoke about the experiment, he emphasized that the activity allowed him to be with friends outdoors, to have fun, and to race against other students. A few weeks after he told us about the experiment, when we asked him about it again, he was able to recall that it was about weight and mass. He described how water balloons behave differently from air balloons, and he said that that was what made them so much fun. He clearly enjoyed the academic side of school at times, something he would never admit to in an interview with us or in conversations we observed him having with his peers. He spoke positively about his own contributions and described this particular teacher as his favorite.

USING THE MARGINS FOR STRENGTH

Living Within Borders

In both these portraits, we begin to see how the lives of homeless youth are lived within the borderland. They are separated from the center by their access to traditional forms of material, social, and human resources, yet they activate nontraditional forms of resources to find other ways of being successful.

Juan and Claudia each attended a poorly resourced, high-poverty elementary school. The teachers in their school underwent a highly popular sensitivity-to-poverty training during the 2 years in which we collected their stories, 1999–2001. However, the very sensitivity training meant to help teachers better cope with the levels of poverty in their school was, in our estimation, discriminatory. On the positive side, the program encouraged teachers to incorporate into their instructional practices the experiences and backgrounds that youth in poverty bring to school. In our talk with teachers this was seen as a valuable message. Most of the teachers felt unsure about what their students' day-to-day experiences were, especially those students in shelters, and held a strong desire to build firmer connections to them. On the negative side, the ways in which their teachers were taught to build these connections further separated Claudia and Juan from those who were not poor.

For instance, the training manual (Payne, 1998) states that teachers should expect wealthy students to "read a menu in English, French and another language" or "know how to read a financial statement and analyze my own financial records" (p. 58), while teachers should expect poor children to know the location of "the churches and sections of town [that] have the best rummage sales," to "know how to get someone out of jail," or to "know how to get a gun" (p. 53). The training manual also states that poor children believe that "personality is for entertainment," that "destiny" is about believing "in fate," and that they "cannot do much to mitigate chance"; whereas wealthy children believe that "personality is for connections," that "financial, political, and social connections are highly valued," and that destiny is "noblesse oblige" (p. 59). Furthermore, the text provides a list of school behaviors "related to poverty," which include laughing when disciplined, arguing loudly with the teacher, making vulgar comments, placing hands on someone else, not being able to follow directions, being extremely disorganized, and being disrespectful to teachers (pp. 103–104).

There are a multitude of other examples in the training program used by Juan and Claudia's school that actively encouraged negative stereotypes about them. The training program appeared to ignore many of the strengths that both Claudia and Juan brought to school. Both were bilingual and could read much more than a menu in Spanish and English. The training manual misrepresented their behavior as being causally associated with poverty. Was Claudia bored with school simply because she was poor? Did Juan choose to draw instead of complete his math assignment because he was poor? Not all teachers bought into this model, and in fact some openly criticized its lack of sensitivity and accuracy. However, we feel it necessary in a chapter on the borderland of youth's lives to draw attention to how teachers were expected to treat their students.

The Borderland as a Place of Strength

Juan's and Claudia's stories are not easy to tell. At their young ages they have experienced separation and discrimination in their attempts to survive. Yet they have refused to live a marginalized life simply because the structures work to limit their academic success and personal freedoms. Both have found ways to create new forms of power, influence, and success among their peers. Although not as successful in traditional academic terms as we might have hoped, Claudia and Juan have used their location on the margin as a place of strength in three significant ways.

First, they use the borderland to *resist the stereotypical and dangerous boundaries that keep them separate from those in power*. There are different kinds of margin and center boundaries that Juan and Claudia have resisted: identity boundaries, resource boundaries, and cultural boundaries. Both critiqued the rules of the shelter and how unfair the application of these stringent rules were for poor families. They relied on the support of their peers and families to resist being labeled inferior or different, to gain access to things to which they might not normally have had access, and to have their ideas used and valued. Juan resisted the label of problem student and often sat quietly in class simply to avoid being noticed. Claudia refused to raise her hand, because she wanted her teacher to know she was bored. Juan agreed with another student who called their school dumb for not doing "real" science activities and for not being able to afford real science equipment. He often hung out with another boy, Junior, when he had community service because Junior knew ways to do community service but still participate in after-school science activities.

Additionally, Juan came to help others value the importance of his carpentry skills in the context of doing science. He became a leader in teaching the other children the skills involved in design and construction, including how to move from two-dimensional figures to three-dimensional models; the importance of mitered boards in putting together a sturdy three-dimensional structure (a challenging spatial relations problem); and using hammers, drills, and other tools. He saw himself as "good" at the tasks involved in building the picnic table. Later, when he recounted in an interview his experiences of the picnic table project, he described as "easy" the process of moving from blueprints and conceptual drawings to models and the final product. This is an interesting statement when contrasted with his negative feelings about his academic success.

Thus, these stories show how the youth use the borderland as a place of strength for survival, success, and avoiding assimilation: learning how to get into and survive the center without being assimilated.

Second, Claudia and Juan used the borderland *as a place of strength for creatively using human, social, and material resources.* We refer here to valuing nonstandard knowledge, experiences, and ways of being in order to achieve something important, and using or gaining access to material resources creatively. The incident of Claudia's desk is a detailed example of how one youth sought to creatively use resources to lessen her own marginalization. Of course, the margin-center separation was sometimes too ingrained in everyday expectations to be resisted or challenged. Although, as noted earlier, Juan came to help others value the importance of his carpentry skills in the context of doing science, he kept strict boundaries around what counted as science, rarely seeing his skills in design or construction as something of value in the more formal science world.

Third, Claudia and Juan used the borderland *as a place of strength for building political solidarity*—for building new and different empowering spaces; for resisting stereotypes, negative expectations, and societal subtexts; and for gaining the strategies to do so. The resulting alliances were forged especially when it meant the youth gained autonomy and access to power. Solidarity was built over unlikely and shifting alliances. We told the tunnel story at the very beginning of Chapter 1. Juan usually never hung out with girls or with younger children (with the exception of one friend, Junior, who was one year younger than he). Yet making the tunnel—a voluntary activity not part of after-school science—had him working closely with both. Claudia has broken written and unwritten rules with the support of her peers in order to have her life reflect the kinds of autonomy and freedom usually granted to youth of her age. If we take a close look at Claudia's story, we can see how she elevated her power and prestige relative to her position as a homeless student with few resources. She was poor and she recognized how poverty limited her access to material resources, but she found friends and teachers who supported her and who valued her expertise.

LOOKING AHEAD

As we reflect on the importance of the margin or the borderland as a place of political solidarity, resistance, and consequence, we are left with many questions: How can we understand how youth use the borderland as a place of strength so that we can connect with them, their desires, and their concerns, especially when we see those desires and concerns reinforcing the boundary work of margin and center? For example, Juan wanted to be a rocklayer because he liked to build and to be outdoors. A rocklayer, according to Juan, was the only job that allowed him to do this. We do not want to devalue his desire to be a rocklayer. After all, he comes from a family in which, for generations, the men have been builders. We want to support his love for his family and encourage his desire to do those things he finds enjoyable.

Yet we believe that it is important to destabilize the boundaries between career trajectories and we want to question the definition of who one must be to follow any particular trajectory. Once we began to see what motivated Juan—what gave him the desire and strength to pursue the idea of the picnic table with his peers—we wondered if we could use that to introduce new ideas and experiences to him. When we told him that architects and engineers are kinds of scientists who also build and spend time outdoors he still seemed not to be convinced. Did Juan understand what we meant? Did he see this as a viable career option? Or were his choices more deeply entrenched in what separated margin and center? We don't want to suggest that these are better options, but we do want Juan to have options.

The borderland is a place of marginality, but it is also a place of strength. It serves as a foundation for the youths' practices of science. In the following chapters, we take a close look at how the borderland serves as a place of strength for the youth in our studies and how they negotiate their identities, relationships, structures, and science events in their lives. We look more closely at how youth co-opt science spaces, at how youth create relevant science practices through the activation of resources in nonstandard ways, at the place of transformations in their lives, and at the role of community places in supporting their actions. The margin, or the borderland, can clearly be a place of despair—a place where homeless youth are positioned by others who view access, power, behavior, and identity as a function of resources. However, as a place of strength and fortitude, it is a place where science can be reimagined to include the lives of youth in urban poverty.

CHAPTER 4

Power and Co-opting Science Spaces

In midspring, we had just completed an ecology study with the students at Hope that left us frustrated. Although we believed that the students were learning about valuable scientific ideas, they seemed to be less engaged than we had hoped. As we prepared to plan a new unit, in order to learn more about our students' interests, we asked each of the students to write a list of "fun things to do in science"; we then hung the lists on the walls of the portable. The students' lists included such things as "catching frogs" and "building a TV." There were some unfeasible ideas, and some that weren't science related, but all ideas were recorded and initially given equal value and recognition.

After talking with the students about their lists, we decided to have them vote on which direction to explore next in after-school science. The idea with the most votes would be the basis for the next science exploration. Before we conducted the actual vote, we wanted to give the children an opportunity to ask questions (of us and of one another) so that they knew exactly what they were voting for. During this time, the children asked one another clarifying questions, such as, "If we made ice cream, could we make any flavor?" Other children used that time to attempt to persuade others to vote for one idea or another. They also asked procedural questions. For instance, Ruben, at age 12 the oldest child in the group, asked if each student could have three votes. We said yes, wrongly assuming that the students would use these three votes to vote for their three favorite ideas.

Ruben took it upon himself to lobby the other children in the group to get them to vote for the topics he wanted to explore—he was interested in bats. Ruben systemically went around first to his brother, Junior, then to his best friends, to get them to cast all three votes for the bats. In the end Ruben corralled enough students to vote for his idea to study bats, although he was successful in only convincing three of his peers to actually cast all their votes for bats. Of course, bats won. Making ice cream came in second.

We then broke into groups—one to plan for bats, the other to plan for ice cream. We quickly learned, however, that Ruben assumed that studying bats implied that live bats would be brought to the shelter. When we explained that we could not bring bats or any other living animals into the shelter because that violated shelter policy, suddenly everyone in that group wanted to change their votes. After all, the ice cream group was going to make real ice cream! The lobbying began again, this time by Ruben and Junior and their friends Jaime and Iris. The new favorite choice was keeping animals as pets—a hamster, gerbil, dog, or cat.

We were frustrated. We had just talked with the students about how it violated shelter policy to have pets—even small pets like hamsters. Yet we were also frustrated that we had to deny the children something that was obviously important to them. We tried to turn the conversation around so that it would go in a productive direction: If we could not have pets to care for, and if we could not bring in live bats to study, what could we do that would allow for the exploration of these same ideas? We offered a few suggestions. We could visit a section of the city where thousands of Mexican free tail bats lived year round. We could also visit the nature center to see living animals in their natural habitat. Our suggestions prompted one student to suggest that we go somewhere where they could explore for different animals and insects. As we found out later, they wanted to capture and keep the insects for their pets. Although having insects as pets seems a strange idea, a couple of the children told us about a classmate who had a pet tarantula and we suspect that this kind of pet was quite intriguing to them.

POWER AND CO-OPTING SCIENCE SPACES

We begin this chapter on co-opting science spaces and power with a story about "fun things to do" for several reasons. First, as teachers, we believed that Ruben used his authority to challenge normative school practices in order to use the fun things to do conversation to convince the group to do what he wanted to do. From his lobbying efforts involving changing the number of votes and encouraging his allies to use all their votes for one idea, Ruben influenced the direction of the conversation and the subsequent direction of after-school science. Second, although we felt to some degree that we were successful in at least responding to Ruben's concerns about what to do next, we also felt as if we were probably not hearing many of the other children's ideas for what to do next. Ruben's active lobbying and rule-changing behavior surprised us, but we allowed it. However, we had not been prepared to understand in some deeply thoughtful ways why he felt it was important to act in the way he did and what this might have meant for our teaching at the moment.

In the previous chapter we discussed the importance of the borderland in learning and doing science. In many ways, transforming power relationships is the crux of life in the borderland. In this chapter, we dig more deeply into themes of power and marginalization and examine issues of power explicitly to see how youth co-opt science spaces to transform the power relations in their lives. In sorting through our data, we have sensed that how youth enact power relations significantly contributes to powerful teaching moments. How kids respond to, act within, and help to shape power relations is important to understand. Thus, in this chapter we focus on the reasons why the youth with whom we have worked do science in their out-of-school lives and the values and beliefs that are central to their practice of science. In particular we respond to the following questions: In what ways do youth interact within the science spaces in their lives? How do power relations frame these interactions? There are two key themes that emerge in this chapter: How and why youth disrupt the structures that frame their engagement with science, and how and when youth disrupt their identities in order to engage in science or to use science to engage in other things. We use these two themes to make a case for the power and importance of youth co-opting science spaces.

POWER AND RESISTANCE

In recent science education studies, the relationship between power and science instruction has been explored through the lens of resistance (Gilbert & Yerrick, 2001; Seiler, Tobin, & Sokolic, 2001, 2003; Tobin, Seiler, & Walls, 1999). There are two important claims to emerge from this literature: that resistance is about exerting control and that resistance is an expression of identity. Undergirding each of these claims is the shared understanding that through acts that are labeled resistant, culture is both produced and reproduced.

Resistance as Control

According to Gilbert and Yerrick (2001), students resist in lower track classes for three primary reasons. They resist having to give up their identities just to succeed (e.g., Black students resist acting "White"); they resist teaching practices that position them as lesser (e.g., students resist the deficit approach to learning); and they resist teacher authority, especially when that authority manifests itself through disciplinary action. What we can read from this study is quite powerful: Student resistance is an active process that students use to make claim to their own space in schools and by which students and teachers negotiate control in schools—control over identity, over what schooling is about, and over relationships and respect.

Tobin and Seiler and their colleagues (Seiler, Tobin, & Sokolic, 2001; Tobin, Seiler, & Walls, 1999) take a perspective similar to that of Gilbert and Yerrick (2001), although the focus of their studies are on high-poverty, African American urban youth. On the basis of sociological studies of cultural reproduction and production, Tobin and colleagues make the case that student resistance, at its heart, is grounded in an opposition to being controlled, and that the purpose of resisting among high-poverty, urban teens is twofold: to disrespect actions or activities that are disrespectful themselves, and to take advantage of opportunities to engage in building a youth-respecting subculture in science class.

As in Gilbert and Yerrick's (2001) study, at issue here is the very notion of control. According to these authors, agents in schools either knowingly or unknowingly control students by framing their participation, effort, and achievement in narrow cognitive terms. Little attention is paid to how cognitive goals (in both form and expression) may be deeply rooted in sociocultural traditions. In other words, the students in Tobin and Seiler's study embed learning in a culture of respect, in which respect ranges from valuing the interests that students bring to the classroom, to utilizing, in classroom-based ways, the primary discursive practices of the students. Such differences in the currency of schooling lead students to act differently from what teachers wish from and for them, even when those wishes are well intentioned. These different actions, which often conflict with "desired" actions, are labeled destructive or resistant.

Resistance as an Expression of Identity

In our own studies with homeless youth and their families (Calabrese Barton, 1998; Calabrese Barton & Yang, 2000), we have drawn on resistance and on cultural production and its connection to the culture of power in science and in school science. In a case study of one young father, Miguel, we showed how, during his teenage years, he resisted the culture of school science while at the same time, as a self-taught herpetologist and businessman, sought to create his own subculture of science in his close-knit neighborhood. For Miguel, resisting school science turned out to be both an act of self-preservation and an act of defiance. Both Miguel's peer culture and the culture of school science were restrictive, demanding conformity to a narrow set of norms and expectations that failed to connect his interests and talents to the wide range of possibilities offered by our society and economy. Miguel was placed in a position of having to choose one over the other. Yet, unlike his peer culture, schooling did *not* provide a safety net of support if he chose to conform to schooling over peer culture. What is particularly interesting to us in this case study is how science itself could have mediated this difference. As a self-taught herpetologist, working in an occupation highly respected among his peers, Miguel possessed the interest and capacity for a practice of science that could have bridged these two worlds.

Thus, in this study about Miguel, as in Tobin and Seiler's (Seiler, Tobin, & Sokolic, 2001; Tobin, Seiler, & Walls, 1999) studies and Gilbert and Yerrick's (2001) work, students appear to resist having their behavior controlled when that behavior appeared to deviate from normative practices in school—how one must talk and act in science class. These studies show us how students produce their own culture by resisting what others want for them. In each of these studies we can also see how resistance and production reflects acts of self-preservation and defiance within a schooling system that defines youth and their science experiences through narrow cognitive goals and specific ways of being.

Limitations of a Resistance Framework

There are two concerns that we bring to this research literature on resistance. The first is that resistance has been framed as an individual activity rather than a community action. In other words, all these studies focus on individual students. But what happens when these students live and work together in science class or at the shelter? How do these different social contexts frame what gets resisted and by whom, and how much this matters to those in charge?

The second concern is that labeling actions as "resistant" is culturally constrained (Seiler, Tobin, & Sokolic, 2003). In other words, student actions labeled as appropriate are actions that fit neatly into what a teacher (or researcher) expects or desires to see. Those student actions labeled as resistant are actions that do not neatly fit what a teacher (or researcher) expects, either because he or she lacks the cultural understandings to make the connection between a student's action and the activity at hand or because the student expresses a different cultural understanding of the activity at hand. Seiler, Tobin, and Sokolic question if our thinking around student resistance might be enhanced if what we view as resistant was further analyzed as a cultural exchange that may or may not produce conflict rather than as a "negative" action that detracts, as is implied by the descriptor *resistant*.

Despite these limitations, these studies together provide a useful framework for understanding how youth actively negotiate power through resistance and production. In particular they share a set of three important assumptions that help to frame any analysis around youth, power, and science education: Youth are authors of their lives and work to generate experiences for themselves that are empowering (at least at the moment and in their local context, though not necessarily long term or in a larger social context). Youth author their lives in relation to the social organizations that structure their lives, and to the cultures that frame those organizations (e.g., schools, science). Those moments to which youth respond in ways that can be read as oppositional ought to be examined more closely and used to challenge our understandings of youth and what they do and believe and our understanding of science and why we do what we do in science education.

POWER AND SCIENCE EDUCATION

In the following section of this chapter, we present stories from two youth: Junior and Iris. These stories focus closely on how these youth negotiated power in science and in their lives, each individually as a member of a larger sociocultural group. The selection of the two youth for this chapter was quite purposeful: We elected to present one girl and one boy, both bilingual and attending the same fourth-grade classroom in a local elementary school, and both regular attendees (with their siblings) of Science Club at the shelter in Well Springs. However, whereas Iris stood out in school as a quiet, well-behaved, high-achieving student (quite like the good-girl stereotype), Junior was a highly disruptive and underachieving student. We wanted to explore if and how their science practices differed in light of our understandings of power and resistance.

In preparing each of the stories, we followed a two-layered approach. First, we developed rich portraits of the youth, including analytic descriptions of their participation in in-school and out-of-school science events. Second, we analyzed their school- and after-school-based experiences and conversations with us to make sense of how power relationships played out in the students' lives, how they shaped their visions of science and their sense of autonomy in doing science. The crosscutting themes presented in this chapter include (a) disrupting structures; and (b) disrupting identity and relationships.

JUNIOR

Junior was in fourth grade when we first met him at Hope Shelter, during the fall of 1999. He was 9 years old and had been living at the shelter for nearly 2 years with his mother and his two brothers—one age 5 and the other 12. Junior attended a local neighborhood elementary school, as did many of his peers at the shelter, although he was looking forward to eventually attending a different school. He believed his school treated the children from Hope Shelter unfairly.

Negotiating Relationships

Although we formally interviewed Junior on three different occasions, talked with his mother and school teachers on many occasions, and hung around with him during after-school hours, we got to know him best through his participation in the after-school science program.

There were many qualities that stood out for us regarding Junior's participation in after-school science, including his constant participation and a willingness to work. One of Junior's most unforgettable attributes, however, was his inclination for openly flagrant commentary. He often had to perform community service as a form of punishment at Hope for cursing and insulting other children. Once, during an interview about his participation in a science project focused on building a picnic table, we asked Junior to tell us more about his participation in the blueprint stage of the picnic table, an activity that occurred between March and July 2000. To this question Junior responded, "Uh, that I smoke weed? Uh, that's not good, right?" During another interview, Junior laughed as he recounted the derogatory "nickname" he had coined for one of his friends. This type of commentary was not uncommon for Junior. In fact, we once arrived at the shelter after he and another child there had had a fight. In this case, it was Junior's remarks on the school bus that had caused the altercation. Junior's comments sometimes led to punishment with community service, but he appeared to enjoy the attention he received when he was isolated from the group by one of the Hope staff. Often this isolation from the larger group would result in Junior's sitting with one of the staff or being assigned tasks around the portable to redirect his attention. Although neither the remarks nor the language Junior used was acceptable to the staff, we believe that his behavior, while disruptive, was his way of seeking adult attention.

The other children at the shelter regarded Junior in quite a positive light. They often laughed at his comments, and they sometimes displayed similar behaviors as a way of gaining acceptance from him. Ironically, Junior's interactions with many of the children were characterized by a certain benevolence toward them. Although they were often the brunt of his jokes, he appeared to be friends with most of his peers. In fact, his interactions with them displayed a certain "coolness"—he was looked up to although he was younger than many of the other children. For example, Juan, a fifth grader at the time, ran into the portable one day during after-school science and said, "Hey, Junior, this guy wants to trade me a [Pokemon] card." Junior responded, "Is it a hologram one?" When Juan answered yes, Junior very calmly said, "Well then, it's a good trade." Juan ran off to trade the Pokemon card.

During the after-school science program, Junior exhibited a wide range of responses to the various science projects. One of the major projects the youth worked on was the design and construction of a full-sized picnic table (see Chapter 5). Junior expressed a great deal of excitement during the building stages of the picnic table, working very hard to make sure that it was secure and well painted. He often wanted to "take charge" whenever there appeared to be a new challenge or problem. For example, when the bolts the youth decided upon for the table ended up being too long, many of the children expressed frustration that the bolts didn't work and that they would have to wait until new, shorter bolts could be obtained. Junior was determined to continue work on the picnic table that day and began corralling his peers around another possible solution—placing the bolts in a new place on the table so that their length did not interfere with other parts of the structure. Although this solution required additional effort— new holes needed to be drilled and new measurements needed to be made to determine how the legs might fit in a different configuration—Junior persevered. However, at times we also witnessed his frustration on certain projects such as the initial sketching activity that required the youth to estimate the dimensions of their proposed picnic table. On the day we first began with the sketches, Junior not only was frustrated with carrying out this task, but also was noticeably disturbed when his older brother, Rueben, measured and sketched these drafts without much trouble.

Although one of the most memorable aspects of Junior's personality was how he often alarmed the adults with the shock value of his remarks, during one interview we began to understand the inner complexity from which these comments came.

> TANAHIA: What kind of things would you change if you could change anything in Hope or in this city?
> JUNIOR: Stop being bad.
> TANAHIA: You would change being bad? Do you think you are bad?
> JUNIOR: Yes.

TANAHIA: When are you being bad?

JUNIOR: Every day.

TANAHIA: And what kind of things do you do when you think you are being bad?

JUNIOR: I fight.

TANAHIA: How could you change those things?

JUNIOR: Just tell somebody to help me.

TANAHIA: Like who?

JUNIOR: Like, my mom.

TANAHIA: Yeah, you could talk to your mom about it and who else?

JUNIOR: Like, everybody, everybody! (*Screaming playfully into the tape recorder*)

TANAHIA: What about the people that you fight, could you tell them that you don't want to fight?

JUNIOR: No.

TANAHIA: Why couldn't you tell them you don't want to fight?

JUNIOR: 'Cause.

After this last comment Junior began singing and talking into the tape recorder so to not have to discuss this matter anymore. We began to realize that although Junior understood that his fighting was not a productive response, he had clearly misunderstood his *actions* as an attribute of himself. Thus, he referred to himself as "being bad" instead of understanding his fighting as a wrong or potentially harmful act. Junior knew that this behavior was undesirable and he wanted to change it. But he also did not want to tell his friends that he did not want to fight. To do so could result in his becoming the object of ridicule. He could also lose the respect that he had garnered at Hope and probably at school as well. His being known as quick tempered was likely an asset that he did not want to lose.

While Junior was subject to the same rules as the other children at Hope, he seemed to find ways to live and work around the rules. He would usually make light of any reprimands from the Hope staff by laughing and making jokes about them. However, in one interview he did speak of the community service that he had to perform as a result of his behavior. Community service, the primary mode the shelter staff used to manage student behavior, was described by one of the children as "being for everything." "Thirty minutes is for bad words. Bad words is for 30 minutes. Fighting is for an hour. Crowd fighting is 2 hours, or an hour and 30 minutes, and throwing things are for 4, 3 hours." When Junior was talking about best and worst things about living at Hope, he described "community service" as the worst. Junior was often known to have community service all week long as a result of a string of misbehaviors from fighting and cursing to littering on the shelter property. Although the penalty of community service sometimes kept children from participating in planned activities, Junior did not seem upset when community service affected his opportunity to participate. In fact, he and some of the other children would often mock the Hope staff by telling one another, "Thirty minutes for you! Thirty minutes for you!" As we will describe later, Junior had devised a scheme for enacting community service in ways that allowed him to participate in those activities he found meaningful.

Whatever the reason for his temperament, Junior was clearly a very helpful and enthusiastic participant in after-school science. When he was immersed in an activity that he enjoyed, he would sometimes make remarks to the other children, but he would often be more concerned with the project. During a project focused on building butterfly gardens, Junior showed a great sense of perfectionism in his construction. When he saw that the wood did not completely cover the bottom portion of the planter, he exclaimed, "Aw, damn, it doesn't fit." He was later comforted in knowing, however, that an opening in the bottom of the planter would allow the excess water to drain. On another occasion, a trip to a small wooded area proved to be the stage for Junior's great display of leadership skills as he led approximately eight other children throughout the stretch in a search for bugs and other small animals.

Once when we asked Junior about his career goals, he remarked that he wanted to be a policeman, a judge, a detective, a soccer player, a science teacher, and a soldier in the army. Later in the semester, we talked to him about his desire to become a policeman. It was at that time that he informed us that his career goal had changed and he now wanted to become a "hammering boy" because he wanted to be able to help people:

TANAHIA: Junior, do you still want to be a policeman?
JUNIOR: Oh, well, well, well, not anymore. I want to be a
    hammering boy to build houses and put the edges on houses.
TANAHIA: OK, why do you want to be that?
JUNIOR: For poor people. For people that are poor.
TANAHIA: So they can have houses?
JUNIOR: Yeah.
TANAHIA: Would you charge them to build the houses?
JUNIOR: No, just $50.
TANAHIA: Just $50? And do you think it's important to build
    houses for people?
JUNIOR: Yeah.
TANAHIA: Why?

JUNIOR: So they can live and not die. Because if they live in the street they are going to die without food.

Undoubtedly Junior's experience with homelessness prompted his sensitivity for those families who are not able to afford shelter.

Learning Science

Junior's science instruction that year was characterized by an absence of experiences in his class. Because of test preparation drill, he and his classmates reported that they did not receive instruction in science. The Texas Assessment of Academic Skills (TAAS) was a major factor in how Junior interpreted his school experience. He spoke about this assessment often and discussed in one interview the effects that TAAS had on his school experience.

> TANAHIA: How does school make you feel?
> JUNIOR: Bad.
> TANAHIA: Why does school make you feel bad?
> JUNIOR: Because we have to do the TAAS.
> TANAHIA: Can you tell me a little more about that?
> JUNIOR: You take it in the fourth grade.
> TANAHIA: And why does the TAAS make you feel bad?
> JUNIOR: Because you don't go to specials.
> TANAHIA: What are specials?
> JUNIOR: When you go to P.E., art, or music, or computers.

Later in Junior's interview we discussed science teaching, and his remarks further uncovered how essential it is to the education of students that teachers, administrators, and policy makers begin to understand the consequences of eliminating subjects from the mandated curriculum.

> TANAHIA: How do you feel about science?
> JUNIOR: It's OK because right now we're building the picnic table and some benches (*referring to after-school science*).
> TANAHIA: OK. How about at school? Can you tell me some words that you use to describe science?
> JUNIOR: We don't do science.
> TANAHIA: And why don't you do science at school?
> JUNIOR: I don't know. Because the teacher, we have a lot of work to do and she does too.

on her. When we asked her if this responsibility bothered her, she just shrugged as if she was not allowed to answer, a gesture possibly indicative of her confusion about who she was and what role to play—child or adult.

Schooling and Science

Iris was an extremely intelligent girl who liked to take on new activities, and often correctly assumed she would perform well at them. Yet sometimes, when presented with even a small obstacle, she immediately questioned the validity of her own choices. When we were nailing posts on signs created by the youth for a nature trail we were building, Iris jumped right in to demonstrate her hammering skills, probably developed in part from an earlier project building a picnic table and bench. She immediately discovered that the grass was too soft to support her work, and she became almost immediately disengaged in the activity. When one of the teachers suggested that she use the pavement as a work surface, which proved useful, she did not want to accept the suggestion and criticized the activity. At the same time, the other children, including her two younger brothers and her cousin Jaime, followed her example both in deed and mood. When Iris showed enthusiasm for something, the other children followed behind. While she did not openly acknowledge this control, we think she enjoyed her leadership role and was excited when adults gave her additional responsibilities. When she suggested making Pokemon characters out of clay that represented different aspects of nature, the other children followed with enthusiasm. Iris did choose, however, to limit how far her ideas were spread for fear of losing control over them. She did not want lots of other children "copying" her ideas and thereby stealing some of her recognition.

In school, Iris's favorite subjects were math, reading, and spelling. When asked why she liked these subjects, she described how she performed well in them. She received A's and A-pluses in reading, and in math, she received 100s on her papers:

> RESEARCHER: What do you like about science or about math and reading?
> IRIS: Math. I always would make hundreds on my math papers.

Like Junior, Iris equated not doing well in school with being bad, describing some students as "good kids" and other students as "bad kids" based on their academic performance.

Iris judged her like and dislike of her teachers based on whether those teachers respected her. She described Ms. J. as her best teacher because she was "nice." She also described how excited she was by a class experiment on weather in which she would have the opportunity to use real chemicals. Here, *favorite teacher* seems to relate to both the kind of relationship and respect she has with and from her teacher and the kinds of opportunities she has to engage in real science experiences.

In discussing her own worst teacher, Ms. R., she described someone who did not understand her situation or her strategies of action. For instance, Iris was often prevented from attending Friday Fun Club at school because of her consistent tardiness on school mornings: "If you get in trouble, then you can't go. If you're late, you can't go. If you're not here, then you don't go. If you're absent."

As Iris described, Friday Fun Club was a program meant to reward students who behaved and completed their assignments. Iris felt that she was unfairly being grouped with the other children who did not behave, when she believed she in fact behaved quite well. Being late for school, according to Iris, was something that she could not help.

The relationship between grades, enjoyment, and respect was central to Iris's understanding of what school was all about. She expressed great frustration that very little science was taught in school "because we have to get ready for TAAS." In fact, even though science was the "tightest" and was her "favorite subject in the whole world," it was not one of her favorite school subjects. She did not see science as a school subject, because they did so little of it in the classroom, and what they did do she felt was boring. When we asked her what it was she wanted her teachers to know about her, if anything at all, she said that she wanted her teachers to know that she "loves science." Even when we pushed her to think of her favorite in-school science activity, since we knew from our visits to her school that she did have some science experiences, she would only list out-of-school activities: "I love science! Like, the most things that I like that we have done was the signs for the nature trail and the picnic table."

When probed to explain more about what she liked about out-of-school science, Iris described several key qualities, including building something that works and having "real" activities, activities that in her words involved "the real thing," such as seeing a "real tornado" rather than making one in a bottle. She also described the importance of working with friends and family. This may help to explain why she liked out-of-school science better than in-school science.

It was not surprising to us that Iris wanted to be a scientist when she grew up. She liked to "discover" things. She felt that her being a scientist would give her an interesting future because science was an important part of life: "Without science they won't be able to get anything from other

autonomy at times to be herself, rather than a stereotype. However, they also seemed sometimes to position her awkwardly among her peers, who, not knowing how to respond, reached for stereotypes to position her as different and consequently with less power in the group. Tracing Iris's participation and resistance in science along these lines was quite interesting. On the one hand, Iris often participated in science to legitimize those less stereotypical qualities about herself (her physical strength and confidence with tools when building the picnic table) in ways that allowed other children to value her leadership rather than to criticize or make fun of her for her "lack" of feminine physical qualities. She also, however, worked to appropriate science activities to value her role as caretaker. As described earlier, Iris initially resisted the building of the picnic table because we had reduced her role as caretaker while simultaneously reducing her brothers' participation in the project. Her resistance in that activity caused us to re-think how and when the younger children should participate in building activities.

Another way in which youth created a practice of science to challenge the connection between identity and power played out in the ways in which the youth participated or resisted science to challenge stereotypes of home-lessness against the backdrop of what it means "to be normal." In popular discourse, homeless people are regarded as lazy and as being able to make it in society if they only worked harder. Junior's desire to become a "ham-mering boy" plays into this finding and helps to challenge how we might better understand and respond to how youth use science to productively confront power. Junior was far from lazy. He worked hard to make him-self noticed. He also worked hard not to be controlled by those who ap-peared to have power over him, even when that meant that his actions would be seen as deviant. Junior described this change of heart in his fu-ture goals because he realized that he could design physical structures that were useful to people, that he was good at building, and that this was some-thing that he could do to prevent others from being homeless.

This example is significant because it shows Junior challenging much larger and much more amorphous power relations. However, for us as science teachers and researchers, Junior's desire to become a hammering boy challenged us at many levels, for we wanted Junior to know that his options for his future could expand beyond the world of manual labor. We also wanted him to see the far-reaching applications of science—to make more real the idea that he could someday be a scientist. How can we work with youth to create a practice of science to challenge complex power rela-tions, while not reproducing social hierarchies? Although, we believed, Junior was quite exceptional in his academic abilities, he struggled to do well in school, and he felt that this made him a bad person. It is interesting to us that although Junior, with adult and peer help, achieved success with both the cognitive dimensions (measurement, scale, design, Hyperstudio communication) and the construction dimensions of the picnic table project, in the end he was influenced most of all by the construction dimensions, in his wanting to become a hammering boy rather than an architect or an engineer.

Another way in which both Iris and Junior struggled to challenge their relative position as high-poverty and homeless youth was their desire to engage in science only if it was "real." Junior reacted strongly when we mentioned to him that his brother described their school as a "dumb school" because "they can't afford nothing" (he was responding to the question of whether he thought that kids should do science projects such as the picnic table in school). Junior agreed with his brother and reiterated that in his school they never do science. Likewise, Iris, who wanted to be a scientist when she grew up, only wanted to do what she called "real science." When we asked her what she meant by a real activity she described it as being something that is "for real," where "you really see it," as in going to see a real tornado rather than building one in a bottle. In the opening story in this chapter, Junior and his brother rejected studying bats once they learned that they could not have real bats to study. In the after-school program, Iris tended to push the group into making the activities "real." When we were building the nature trail, Iris and her younger brother were initially quite excited about the project. They were interested in nature and spoke often about a love for animals. The two siblings had heard that deer lived on the golf course down the street from the shelter. In preparing for the nature trail, we tried to secure property for the trail in the undeveloped land near the golf course. However, when Iris and her brother learned that the nature trail was not going to be near the golf course—that it was going to be in the informal dumping ground right next to the shelter (and an area that the adults would have to clean up before it was safe for students), they both vocally criticized the nature trail project as a "stupid" activity. They believed that there was no wildlife in the dumping area, and it did not make sense to them that they would build a nature trail where there would be no wildlife.

CO-OPTING SCIENCE SPACES

Disrupting structures and identities allowed the youth to reposition themselves with respect to authority and to "take control" over the spaces in which science learning happened in their lives. Junior and Iris had multiple opportunities to do science and multiple barriers that prevented their participation in science. Yet both managed to participate in science. Both co-opted science spaces in order to experience fun and belonging, to live up to their own and others' expectations, and to legitimate those aspects of their lives that were actively marginalized by larger social regulations. Co-opting science spaces—what happens when youth disrupt the structures and identities that frame their participation in science—is, therefore, an important practice in their efforts to learn science and to be respected, valued, and powerful in that process.

As discussed in Chapter 2, science spaces are the social environments in which science gets done. These social environments are dynamic places influenced by the participating individuals, the rules and expectations for participation, the tools typically employed in that shared participation, the artifacts produced there, and both macro and micro structures.

We intentionally have chosen the word *co-opt* to describe how youth claim authority in science spaces. Conventionally, to co-opt something is to adopt or appropriate something as one's own. By suggesting that youth co-opt science, we are making the assertion that they are claiming mastery over science and a set of strategies of action that are acceptable within science domains whether or not these have historically been accepted.

Looking closely at how youth disrupt structures and identities reveals that youth's abilities to co-opt science spaces depends on two criteria:

- Their ability to adopt the intended purposes of that space and to transform it to their advantage
- A sophisticated level of understanding of the rules and cultures that govern that space, and a desire to challenge them on the grounds of fairness

In reference to this second criterion, the youth were particularly critical of the social arrangements that determined participation in science, rules that determined what actions were allowable, and opportunities to learn and do real science.

Embedded within each of the ways in which youth co-opt science (see Table 4.1) are the primary ways in which the youth drew on the resources available to them to co-opt science. They drew on their knowledge of science, including scientific ideas and concepts; science processes; the language of science; their knowledge of how the system works; their allies, both peers and adults; and the resources available to them.

In particular, we noted that when challenging structures, they activated the human capital of knowledge of how the system works, including an understanding of the implicit and explicit rules for participation and of the discursive practices that are acceptable within those systems. They

Table 4.1. Co-opting Science Spaces

	Strategies	Structures and Resources Drawn upon by Youth
Adopting science spaces for multiple purposes	Giving multiple meanings to scientific activities Using scientific tools and materials for nontraditional and sometimes subversive activities Doing "acceptable scientific activities" to create a sense of normality	Knowledge of science, including scientific ideas and concepts, science processes, and the language of science Knowledge of how the system works Forming new and strategic alliances with peers
Challenging relationships and structures that determine when, how, and why science gets done	Being critical of social arrangements that determine participation in science and rules that determine what actions are allowable Opportunities to learn and do real science Pedagogy in the classroom	Knowledge of how the system works, including understanding the implicit and explicit rules for participation Appropriate discursive practices Finding allies among other peers and adults and working with them to win a cause

also activated their social capital of seeking out allies or those peers and adults who would help them to challenge a rule or a structure or to limit the severity of any sort of reprimand that might be associated with such a challenge. They also activated their personal conviction that when something is unfair, they have a right and a responsibility to articulate and act against that unfairness, even if that meant they might get in trouble.

Youth co-opt science spaces all the time for multiple personal goals—to be with friends, to play and do something different from just book learning, and to try out different kinds of identities. For example, if we return to the story presented in Chapter 2, we can see Kobe's participation in Community Day as multipurposed: He had an opportunity to work on the project by helping to build the fence and plant the garden. He brought his

CHAPTER 5

Relevant Science: Activating Resources in Nonstandard Ways

THE BEGINNINGS OF A PICNIC TABLE

Claudia's desk (see Chapter 3) opened up to the students at Hope Shelter a whole new set of possibilities about what could happen in Science Club, and this potential was powerful among the students. Claudia's creativity and autonomy in deciding to make a desk instead of a planter hardly went unnoticed by the other participants in the after-school science program. In particular, Junior, the vivacious 9-year-old portrayed in Chapter 4, had suggested building a playhouse at several points during the semester, and now, after our having seen Claudia's success, his idea began to look like a real possibility. Demonstrating his skill as a charismatic leader, Junior's older brother, Ruben, took it upon himself to advance his brother's idea. He began talking with the other children about how their next big project ought to be "building a clubhouse." After all, they had built planters and Claudia had built a desk. According to Ruben, a clubhouse was vital, for it would be designed and constructed by the children specifically as "a space for kids." Given the play space restrictions on the children, and given that each of the families at Hope lives in a one-bedroom apartment, the club-house was envisioned as a way to provide the students with some much coveted and well-deserved personal space, a "kids only" area that was truly theirs: theirs to design, build, and use outside the authority of their par-ents, teachers, and social workers. The clubhouse emerged as the youth started to realize that they could exercise their own senses of agency and as we started to better understand the powerful science activities that could emerge when we allowed the students to do so.

Ruben's efforts to advance the idea of a clubhouse seemed to be well calculated. He had amassed a strong set of evidence for why the clubhouse was necessary: The children needed a place to play any time of the day, they needed a place to store their things, and they needed privacy. He believed that the building should be expansive and permanent, unlike the Children's Activity Portable, which was old, cramped, and not made to last. He had an explanation for how the task could be accomplished. They would need lumber, nails, hammers, saws, drills, and other tools and materials. Some of the children could cut the wood, others could hammer, and still others could paint and decorate. He used his ideas to make the concept of building a clubhouse appealing to individual children. As he lobbied the other children, he helped them to see their "place" in the clubhouse. We remember hearing him tell Juan that he could be one of the main builders. This was extremely perceptive of Ruben, because although Juan was a student whose participation in Science Club was inconsistent, he had seemed much more engaged than usual when the students were building planters. As Juan said of himself, building was what he was expert at. Furthermore, the more Ruben talked about the clubhouse, and the more students he tried to encourage to buy into his idea, the more sophisticated his vision of the clubhouse became. Eventually he set upon building not just any clubhouse, but a three-story clubhouse. The first floor would be for the "little kids" who would have a place to play while not having to share their space with the bigger students. Then the older girls and the boys could split the second and third floors. Ruben believed that the boys should have the third floor, but this was a highly contentious point and one that we don't believe the children ever resolved.

The student's enthusiasm about building a clubhouse was obvious and we discussed the idea with the decision makers at Hope Shelter. Unfortunately, a permanent clubhouse was frowned upon, in part because Hope intended to expand into the outdoor spaces currently being used by the children's program, and in part out of concern for the students' physical safety. We agreed on the safety issue. It was one thing to build garden planters or even a desk. It was quite another to build a clubhouse, especially one that was three stories tall!

Rather than deny the students their project, though, we had another conversation about what the students might like to build in place of a clubhouse. It seemed to us that building something for their play space was important to them. A clubhouse might have been out of the question, but there were plenty of other things that could be built. Determined to see their clubhouse become a reality, however, the students, led by Ruben, redirected our conversation from things to build *instead of* the clubhouse into things to build *for* the clubhouse.

Building for the Clubhouse

This shift from what to build instead of the clubhouse to what to build for the clubhouse was subtle, yet captured the spirit of Ruben's and several of

protective of Ruben. No one was allowed to make fun of him, and children new to the shelter quickly learned this unwritten rule. He was not, however, immune to other kinds of sparring, such as in conflict around friendships, clothing, or school behavior. It was simply that his illness was never allowed to be the overt focus of attention. Once, when he was hospitalized for 2 weeks, we asked a social worker at the shelter about his illness. She admitted that she knew very little about what afflicted Ruben and that his mother kept this information quite private.

Ruben confided in us that he was not very enthusiastic about entering junior high that next fall. He felt that the older and larger students would tease him because of his size. He had expressed some resentment when his younger brother, Junior, had surpassed him in height earlier that year.

Ruben's physical frailness did not curtail his social or intellectual life. This 12-year-old was very outspoken and had well-developed leadership skills. The Hope staff often looked to him to gather and assist the younger children. He also assisted the Hope staff in translating English to Spanish for the younger kids, since he was fluent in both languages. The other children at the shelter seemed to look to him for acceptance and guidance; they often asked his opinion on the pictures they drew or things they made in the program. When Ruben suggested an activity, most of the students agreed that it would be "cool." The younger children especially looked up to him for assistance when doing after-school science projects.

Ruben was rather astute in how he enacted his leadership among his peers. Many of the projects we did in Science Club were his ideas or offshoots of his proposals. For instance, when the children were debating where to place the butterfly garden, Ruben was adamant that the garden sit just west of the Children's Activity Portable, next to the tall black fence. He was quite passionate in his reasoning. He argued that beside the portable would be the best location for the butterfly garden because it would be out of a high-traffic area, and it would get plenty of sunlight and enough shade. The other students, who had other ideas for locations, seemed to be quickly persuaded by Ruben's insight. Once he "won" the location, he urged his peers to go outdoors to mark off the space with rope, even though the garden wasn't to be built for several more weeks, and they agreed to this, too.

Among Ruben's other fine qualities were his sense of adventure and his resourcefulness. He showed tremendous interest in animals and archaeology. He was always a vocal advocate for studying and caring for snakes, looking for spiders, digging in the earth, and raising small animals. He often sat and read the field guides and other materials we brought with us each week. Occasionally, he would ask to borrow a book for a week. Once, while digging in the earth and trying to find small animals that lived there, Ruben began recalling some of the names of beetles that he had read about in a field guide. He appeared to have a genuine interest in science, both traditional forms and the more practical approaches implemented in Science Club. In fact, his career goals were either to become an "archaeologist, astronomer, or to work on computers." However, when Tanahia asked him about college, he abruptly answered, "I ain't going to college." After Tanahia expressed to Ruben that in college he could learn many of the things to aid him in his chosen career, such as how to conduct an archaeological dig, he seemed less against the idea of higher education.

Ruben's astuteness and love of science did not always translate well into his academic performance. In fact, he appeared to be indifferent toward school. His responses to schooling were usually based on two criteria: his grades and his relationship with his teacher. Although he often talked about math and science as being his favorite school subjects, he also reported that his least favorite subjects were math and social studies because he made low grades in them. Ruben further stated that he thought he could have made better grades in these areas if his teacher had "explained [the information] longer." It was interesting to see the tension between Ruben's favorite and least favorite school subjects. Perhaps he enjoyed these subjects but the fact that he did poorly in them caused him to have mixed emotions about them. However, he stated that he participated in "special tutoring on Mondays and Wednesdays," in an attempt to improve his performance.

On his report card, Ruben consistently received B's, although he did receive A's in physical education and C's in collaboration and group work. However, his math grades took the path of a roller coaster, ranging between C's and A's. He did not have a defeatist attitude when he discussed his performance, however. He felt that if he worked harder, he could, in fact, do better in these subjects. We wondered how much the absences caused by his illness contributed to his fluctuating math grades, in a class that, in his school, relied heavily on daily worksheets.

Power and Identity

Ruben appeared to be everyone's "big brother." He was rarely involved in confrontations with the other students. When students would attempt to challenge him, he would often use verbal force rather than fight physically, and he was almost always successful in ending any standoffs with other students. When Ruben did engage in confrontation, it was usually because he believed an injustice was being served. He was quick to point out when situations were unfair or "wrong." And when he wasn't listened to, he would sulk. Most of the time, however, when Ruben believed something was unfair or wrong, he took matters into his own hands and dealt with the consequences later. More than we did any other child at Hope, we witnessed Ruben engaging in these kinds of activities that were confrontational (toward authority) but solidarity building (with peers) at the shelter, at school, and in after-school science.

For instance, while working on the planters, we had noticed that Ruben was absent that day from Science Club. We were surprised because when we first arrived at the shelter, we had talked to Ruben and knew he was around, and he rarely "skipped" Science Club. Nor did his brother, Junior, know where he was. Some time later, one of the Hope staff came over and began to reprimand the children, saying that it was against shelter policy to have friends over. She was quite forceful in her delivery and understandably so, for it was her job to help secure the premises for the families at the shelter. We quickly discovered that it was because of Ruben that she had made this announcement. He had invited one of his friends from school over to play on the computers. This was a defiant act, for Ruben was well aware of the rules of the shelter. In the interviews, he communicated more than once his displeasure at not being able to spend time with his friends.

> TANAHIA: Can you tell me about Hope—some words you would use to describe living here?
> RUBEN: I do not like living here.
> TANAHIA: Why?
> RUBEN: Because it's boring and you can't go anywhere.
> TANAHIA: Where are some places you would like to go?
> RUBEN: With my friends.
> TANAHIA: With your friends? Where do your friends live? Do they live around the school or far away?
> RUBEN: Kind of far.

There were several factors in the shelter environment that could have diminished Ruben's feelings of power. First, he was unable to invite friends to the shelter. Although these rules were in place for his protection, he understood them as controlling mechanisms that kept his friends away. When he did attempt to invite a friend over despite the rules he was reprimanded. The very fact that Ruben did invite his friend to the shelter showed a tremendous amount of will and courage. We believe that his actions were not malicious, but rather reflected a desire to ignore those rules that seemed to further alienate his friends or himself from normal adolescent experiences.

At Hope, there was a small computer room equipped with four individual stations, offering the only computers at the site. Ruben enjoyed surfing the Internet for Pokemon and Dragon Ball Z sites and playing various computer games. Since most of the families at the shelter lacked such personal resources as computers, going to the computer lab was one of the favored activities of the young residents. One particular afternoon, the kids were working on "biosketches," short biographies with digital pictures of themselves. Ruben told one of us (Tanahia) that he did not want to complete a biosketch because he would rather go online. Tanahia told him that it was OK for him to do so. Some time later, she heard a loud noise and looked over to see Ruben repeatedly slamming a desk drawer. After talking with him, she found out that he was upset because he could not find any of the staff members to key in the code that would allow him to go to unapproved sites. The computer system at Hope was very guarded. All sites required a password the first time they were accessed, as a way to monitor what students view. Even children's or educational Web sites were restricted and required an administrator's code to enter. As a student clicked on a link to the site or a different page on the same site, a box appeared, asking for the code again. This could happen multiple times on the same site and it infuriated the children. Now, as we reflect on Ruben's frustration and his actions on that day we see how fed up he must have been—having only limited time on the computers and being so restricted in where he could look for information.

To Ruben, it seemed that every aspect of his life was governed by rules that he had no part in making. When we discussed his experiences at school, Ruben expressed frustration as he reflected on one of his teachers.

> RUBEN: My homeroom teacher I do not like him. And my math
>   teacher I do.
> TANAHIA: And why don't you like your homeroom teacher?
> RUBEN: He's mean to us. I went to the office today because of him.
> TANAHIA: And why did you go to the office?
> RUBEN: Because I didn't do my sentences that I had to do today.
>   Oh, and he was going to send me to BMC [behavior
>   modification counseling].
> TANAHIA: What's BMC?
> RUBEN: It's when you go all day and stay and do your work by
>   yourself and sometimes other kids are there but you can't talk.

After interviewing and talking informally to the students at Hope, we found that many of them had also been sent to BMC. While BMC was not feared or dreaded by the students, a feeling of despondency resulted from having being sent there. For Ruben, it was not anger, but frustration, that he showed after having to sit in the room all day for not writing sentences.

Thus, Ruben was an intelligent, resourceful, creative, and highly influential boy among his peers. He had a strong desire to see fairness win out, even if that meant going against the rules or getting in trouble. For him, fairness was a complex ideal. It did not mean everyone should get the same thing or be able to participate in the same way. Fairness was more about allowing events, activities, or behaviors even when they were forbidden, if they contributed to some sense of "normality" or what he believed all children should have and experience. Most of the time, when Ruben sought fairness, he was respectful of authority and tried to get his idea of what should happen to fit within established parameters, such as when he wanted to build for, rather than instead of, the clubhouse, or when he wanted to do science activities on the computer so that he could use the Internet. He was not always successful, as the computer story suggests, and Ruben found himself in trouble quite often.

RELEVANT SCIENCE AND THE PICNIC TABLE

We have chosen to highlight Ruben's story in a chapter about relevant science, the activation of resources, and the picnic table because it was Ruben's leadership that convinced the other children and us to build a table and chairs. He had witnessed Claudia's desk and used that observation to insist that a clubhouse was possible. He had ideas about how all the different children could (and should) participate and clearly articulated reasons for why it was necessary to do so. In short, Ruben's involvement in the picnic table project illustrates the means by which relevant science is partly constructed through the activation of resources in nonstandard ways. In particular, we explore two ideas:

- Intersections of human and material capital—new forms of expert knowledge, skills, and capabilities
- Intersections of social and human capital—authorship as a community practice

In the following section of this chapter, we return to the rest of the picnic table story and use it to address and describe these two ideas. Although we have centered much of the story around Ruben, we have also highlighted the participation of several of his peers.

NEW FORMS OF EXPERT KNOWLEDGE, SKILLS, AND CAPABILITIES

Being an Expert: Designing and Building the Picnic Table

After producing conceptual drawings for the furniture to be built for a future clubhouse, the students made balsa wood models of their favorite two drawings to better understand the real constraints and details that would face them during construction. For this activity, the students worked in groups and produced two models. Jaime took primary responsibility for assembling one of the models (see Figure 5.3). The top of his group's model table consisted of four pieces of wood, approximately eight inches long, that were glued to one another along their long edges. Four legs, each about three inches long, were attached at the corners of this resulting rectangular board, supporting the tabletop and creating the form in which many tables are constructed (with the legs normal to the plane of the table, geometrically speaking). Ruben and Iris led a second group in building a model that looked more like a traditional picnic table, complete with two benches (see Figure 5.4). Here, the students confronted several interesting design questions, such as how to attach the legs to the tabletop and how to miter the bottoms of the crossed legs so that they would sit flat on the ground. Once both models were complete, the students evaluated the two designs. In the end they chose the more traditional picnic table design, but not sim-

Figure 5.3. Jaime's picnic table model (flat design).

Figure 5.4. Ruben's picnic table model (traditional mitered design).

ply because it looked more like a picnic table. In our discussions, students considered how easy or difficult it would be to build the table, its aesthetic qualities, its overall proportional size, and its mobility. They also considered how stable both designs were and whether the table would withstand the rather rough treatment that it might face as a piece of outdoor furniture in the children's play area. If it was going to be around for any length of time, the legs would have to be secure. The students decided that the legs on the more traditional table would give the needed stability "because they're crossed and they won't fall."

Once the students selected their favorite model, we asked them to generate a list of supplies that they would need to begin the actual construction. We had asked them for very specific information about the supplies they needed: size (three-dimensional measurements of lumber, length and diameter of nails), quantity, color (when appropriate), and purpose for the supply. Ruben and Iris, the two older students who led in the creation of the winning model, with the help of Junior and Jaime, were quick to take the lead in generating this list. Their dynamics in generating the list is worth noting. This happened near the end of the afternoon, and there were only four students working on the list with Angie while the rest of the students went to play, knowing that Iris and Ruben would probably get the task done. None of the four seemed to mind that the other children left them and quickly added items to the list: wood, paint, nails.

We pushed them to be more specific about these items: What kind of wood do you want? How can you find this out? What size? How many pieces? They struggled with these questions. None of the students had ideas about what kind of wood they should use—in fact, they were a little surprised that the question was even asked, and that there were different kinds of wood to consider. In response, one of the students stated that they should use wood from a tree, suggesting that he understood all wood from trees to be the same in quality. After talking about the different kinds of tree wood (as well as other kinds of wood, such as compressed particle board), Ruben stated that he did not care what kind of wood they used as long as it was weatherproof (could stand up to rain and sun) and sturdy (could stand up to the wear and tear of daily use). Iris added that she didn't want the wood to be so hard that it would crack when they tried to send nails through it.

Ruben used the balsa wood model to figure out how many pieces of wood were needed and their relative sizes. He counted the number of pieces of balsa wood strips used in the model to determine the actual numbers of pieces of wood for the real table. For its size, he estimated that the table should be about 10–15 times larger than the model, and then generated actual measurements for the wood based on the actual size of the model. However, Ruben deferred to Iris's judgment about nails, screws, and so on, as she referred to her experience with her grandfather to provide specifics. Although Iris did not have the language to name the kinds of nails, nuts, and bolts she believed were needed, she was able to describe what these items looked like and how many she thought we should get.

Iris's expert knowledge, derived from her experiences with her grandfather, came into play over and over again during the project. One of the key challenges to arise in the actual building of the table was how to get the long bolts through the cross-sectional piece of wood that held the tabletop together and into the table legs. The children had measured the length of the bolt, lined up the table legs with the tabletop, and carefully marked where the drill should enter the wood and where it should exit. What they had not anticipated was what would happen to the spacing of one table leg when the first leg was already attached to the table. The problem they ran into was that one leg would actually be set back by two inches (the width of the other leg) because the legs crossed. A couple of the youth seemed disheartened until Iris came up with a solution. She suggested that the bolt be removed and be screwed in from the opposite direction, and that an extra piece of wood be added by the table leg so that there would be some extra stability. This was not part of the original plan, and although Jason helped Iris figure out exactly how to add that extra piece of wood, she had clearly

Figure 5.5. Assembling the picnic table.

Figure 5.6. Ivy's sign.

Figure 5.7. Painted picnic table model.

again later over the several weeks of building the picnic table. In fact, he would sometimes oversee construction, once stepping in to help a younger student, saying, "I'm good at this." So to some degree, these activities connected with Juan's identity: he saw himself as proficient in building and construction tasks. When he grew up, Juan wanted to work as a "rocklayer," and own his own business, saying he would "buy a truck, get some tools, go all over the world. Go to Canada, China, go everywhere. Go to Houston, Dallas."

Junior, who originally pushed the idea of building the clubhouse, also was affected by his building experiences. When we first met him, he wanted to be a policeman when he grew up but then after helping to build the picnic table changed his career goals to become a hammering boy. Junior and his family had been living at Hope for nearly 2 years at this time. Combined with his experiences in construction activities, his own situation of homelessness would seem to have led to at least a moment of empowerment, in which Junior saw himself as having the potential to help other poor families without homes. Likewise, in an interview after the picnic table had been built, Juan, a fifth grader, expressed his belief that the picnic table project was not science, because "making things isn't science," but rather, "construction."

Junior's and Juan's responses were telling; they suggested to us that what they most connected with in the picnic table experience was the build-

required in creating relevant science: Claudia showed us that our ideas about science activity were not always relevant; Juan showed us that activities that were relevant are not always seen as scientific: Ruben showed us that science activities could be made to be more relevant when we broadened our own perspectives on what relevancy meant. What other experiences, knowledge, and skills were important to students and how might we know?

For example, we believe that there are three sets of important questions to consider when we reflect on what students are learning in addition to standard knowledge: In terms of the nature of science, how do students see themselves as users and producers of science, in ways that reflect the life of their communities alongside the worlds of science? In terms of the role of science in creating change, how do children take responsibility for the science that they do, for the ways in which they connect science to their community, and for how they integrate their feelings and beliefs into their scientific investigations? In terms of authority, how do youth use real-life problems to make a case for why certain science projects should be done? These questions (summarized in Table 5.2) point toward something different from but complementary to a list of concepts, theories, or skills that youth need to know, for they suggest how knowing science might be understood as an integral component of one's life. Taken seriously, the call for scientific literacy for all compels us to create learning opportunities so that all individuals can use science to empower themselves and their communities. Part of this process certainly includes what students know, while another part includes how that knowledge is integrated into one's life.

AUTHORSHIP AS A COMMUNITY PRACTICE

Authorship of the Picnic Table

Also interesting was the way in which students viewed "authorship" or "ownership" of the picnic table. In connection with the construction of the picnic table and benches themselves, some students decided to use extra wood to make signs that would accompany the table. Most of the signs expressed students' desire to share the picnic table with the rest of the shelter community: Signs read, "Have a great time!" and "Enjoy yourself!" The children knew that others would be able to use the picnic table, and the signs reflected a concern about how people would treat it. Ivy made a sign that read, "Don't vandalize, just relax," because she didn't want others to "write on it" and "mess it up." Other students agreed, saying that

Table 5.2. Learning from the Picnic Table: What Else Do Students Learn?

	Relevant Science	Questions for Assessment: What Students Know/Learn/Do
Relevant science: the nature of science knowledge	Scientific knowledge is a humanmade explanation of how the world works, and is thus subjective, yet rigorous and reflexive. Concepts, although rigorously tested, are culturally based and need-based explanations of natural phenomena to be applied in everyday life activities. Science teaching and learning should include the content, process, histories, norms for participation, and discursive practices. Students should be viewed as users and producers of science.	What content, process skills, and habits of mind do the children develop? How do these reflect the national and state standards for children their age? In what ways do the children see the science that they do as emerging from their needs, desires, concerns, etc. (in how their science questions/ projects are conceived)? In what ways do the children perceive the science they do as reflecting their daily realities (language, culture, race, home life, and community life)? Efficacy in science: How do the children see themselves as users and producers of science, and how interested, motivated, and involved are they in the project (in the day-to-day activities, in the long-term project, a year after the project)?
Relevant science: the role of transformation and power	Science is a social activity and involves understanding of how human values and characteristics shape scientific knowledge and understanding. Science has an ethical responsibility for the knowledge it produces about the world. The teaching and learning of science ought to contain elements of action and change—learning is not just an academic task; it is about interacting with/in the world.	How do the children intentionally link the science they do with their perceived personal needs? with community needs? How do the children integrate their feelings and personal concerns and community values and cultures into the science they do? How do the children take responsibility for the science that they learn and do?
Relevant science: the role of authority	Scientific concepts emerge from dealing with societal problems, real life, and the needs of the local community, which are seen as fundamental to the creation and production of science.	How do the children use science to identify societal and real-life problems and the needs of the local community? How do the children use real-life problems to make a case for why certain science activities or projects should be done?

people who weren't involved in building the table might "make it all wob-bly . . . and it could fall down," in which case "we'll have to do it all over." Another sign included a list of the names of people who had contributed to building the picnic table. This sign was surprisingly controversial among the students. Some supported it because it showed who was involved. As Ivy noted, when someone saw the sign, "they could know who did the picnic table and the chairs."

By contrast, some students recognized that not everyone whose name was on the sign had participated to the same degree and that not everyone who could use the picnic table would actually be included on the sign. For these reasons, Ruben suggested it was better not to have that particular sign at all. During a group interview about the picnic table, the students were discussing pictures that they had taken to document the project. When attention turned to the picture of the name sign, Ruben opposed the sign, saying that other students who were represented on the sign had not con-tributed equally. He believed that others "don't need to know who built it." One hypothesis we have about why this would be the case was that Ruben's 4-year-old brother, Rigo, came by one afternoon while we were building the picnic table, although he was too young to "officially" par-ticipate in Science Club. Ruben was always very protective of Rigo, and we believe that some of his negative feelings about the sign resulted in part from a concern that since Rigo's name had not been included, he would not be allowed to enjoy it once it was completed. It seems that for both sides in this minor dispute over the name sign, the picnic table was a source of pride for the students. It was something they themselves had built and they wanted recognition for their efforts, but it was also an improvement that they had made for the benefit of their families and members of the shelter community, all of whom were welcome to enjoy it equally, regardless of their "official" participation.

Four students were charged with communicating information about the picnic table project to the broader community. To do so, they made HyperStudio presentations that told the story of the picnic table. We started these presentations during one of our weekly meetings, and returned the following week to learn that two of the students, Iris and Junior, had cho-sen to spend several hours of their free time during the week working on their presentations in the computer room. They had each created presen-tations of more than 20 pages, complete with pictures, descriptions, color-ful backgrounds, and fancy navigation between cards. It was interesting to note that the content of each one of the HyperStudio presentations in-cluded more pictures and text about people who worked on the project than about the picnic table itself. Just as the signs raised questions about the picnic table's role in the community, these presentations seem to point to the importance of inclusion and community in the students' practices of science. That is, when Iris and Junior told the story of the picnic table project, they were less concerned about the details of design and construction than they were about the people who helped make their idea a reality.

Furthermore, in one of our recorded conversation with Iris, we talked with her about what made the picnic table a good science project. Her response was twofold: she could nail and hammer, and it gave the children a place to eat and play. Although she does mention the model building and the conceptual drawings as part of the process, her attention is much more focused on the nonscience aspects of the project.

For almost a year, the picnic table remained central to the youth's after-school lives. It was the only piece of outdoor furniture in the fenced-off area by the portable building. The table was amazingly sturdy and well used as an activities table, as a place to eat, as a platform for peering over the fence that marked the shelter boundary, and as "home base" in outdoor games. When new students would move to the shelter, they would sometimes ask about the picnic table. The students who were involved in the project seemed to enjoy explaining that "we built it," to which the new students often showed their admiration by turning to one of the teachers and asking, wide-eyed, "Really?"

RELEVANT SCIENCE

All the stories we have told in this book have left us with similar questions about the ways in which science and youth's lives intersect. When unpacking these stories, we began to see how the students' interest and enthusiasm drove the redefinition of the science activity that we as teachers had planned. In the case of Claudia's desk, we saw how a science event gave her a space in which to exercise and develop her identity as an individual capable of making changes in her life. In our trying to apply these observations to our ongoing work with youth, it seemed to us that science teaching ought to acknowledge and reflect how science activity grows from and redefines the worldviews of participants. Translating such a global objective as performing "relevant science" into daily practice is difficult. We have found that by examining how and when youth activate resources in nonstandard ways, we could begin to see what makes science events relevant.

Clearly, the children valued—and needed—different forms of knowledge to be successful in their efforts to build a picnic table. They needed knowledge that looked like "more formal science knowledge" such as measures, scale, spatial relationships, and movement from models and representations to actual objects. The students drew blueprints. They con-

spond to those questions, and in having the freedom to draw from the work of other scientists and to be critical of that work.

In this chapter we have argued that one way to begin to be more mindful in our attempts as researchers and teachers is to think hard about what it means to engage students in relevant science. However, we are left with many questions. What are we missing? That is, what kinds of additional teaching and research efforts are necessary to really begin to understand whether a relevant science approach is an effective way to generate more equitable, relevant, and empowering science education for all students? Given the degree to which this is fundamentally grounded in the lives and contexts of students, can it become part of the typical kinds of prepackaged curricula found in schools across the country, or does it mean that all science teachers must each build his or her own individual science curriculum? Would this be realistic, given the nature of schooling and the teacher's role in that process? Although these questions can be overwhelming, we believe that such an approach holds power in making science more equitable, more relevant, and more empowering for all students.

CHAPTER 6

Transformations: Science as a Tool for Change

In Chapters 4 and 5 we examined the ways in which youth transformed the science spaces and the activation of resources for science in their lives. In presenting one story in detail, "Darkside and the Community Garden," we build on these themes to make a case for how youth's practices of science are intertwined with using science as a formative tool for generating personal change and community change. In particular, we look at two kinds of transformations: transformations of science and transformation of youth worlds.

GETTING TO KNOW DARKSIDE

An Agent of Change

Darkside, a 16-year-old self-labeled Black Cuban American, stood in front of a small video camera in the middle of a half-finished community garden in an inner-city New York neighborhood. Darkside had been working with his peers for approximately 8 months in an after-school science program to build the garden in an abandoned lot across the street from the shelter where he lived. Alongside the lot project, he also had been working with two other teens to produce a video, titled *The Urban Atmosphere*, about science and life in the inner city.

The last scene, filmed in the garden, was intended to provide a sense of what doing science could mean for inner-city youth and their communities. The plan was to have each of the three teens share their final thoughts on the lot project—to describe what they set out to do, what they accomplished, and why such actions were important to them. Darkside spoke first in this final scene. His presentation style, as he opened the final scene, was calm, even, and full of factual detail regarding his particular involvement:

ing to Live and **Work Within Schools and Shelters**

e time I (Angie) got to know Darkside he had been living in city-run
eless shelters with his mother, father, and brother for more than
rs, and most recently at Southside Shelter for 1 year. He was 15 years
in the 10th grade, and had plans to graduate from high school, go to
ege, and "make something out of his life." Darkside was not exactly
e what he wanted to do with his life, but he emphatically believed it
s important to leave his options open by getting a good education and
oiding gangs:

> I plan to graduate from high school and go to college. I want to
> make something out of my life. Do some good. I don't belong to
> gangs. My mother doesn't want me to. It's been hard on her—my
> older brother died and my other older brother is incarcerated for
> gang-related activity. Not being in gangs is hard because even
> though you stay away from violence, you also don't get their
> protection.

Darkside worked well in collaboration with others, as he did when it
came to the after-school science program. However, he was also fiercely
independent. He did not appear to need the approval of his peer group
for whatever beliefs or actions he pursued, even when failing to seek approval meant that he would be punished for not doing so. As the preceding quote illustrates, one of the ways in which his independence played
itself out was through his efforts to remain gang-free even though his efforts to stay away from gangs made schooling difficult. Within the social
structuring of schools such as Darkside's, gangs were sources of conflict
and safety. For example, in the winter of 1998, Darkside was chased by
several teens and accidentally tripped, breaking his leg. He was in a full
leg cast for 8 weeks and required several additional weeks to rebuild leg
strength once the cast was removed. During this time period Darkside refused to attend school out of fear for his own safety and his mother encouraged him in this decision.

His teachers sent home his assignments each week, but most assignment packages were thin, containing only math and vocabulary worksheets. Although Darkside complained that his teachers were not sending
complete assignments home, he put little effort into completing and returning assigned work. Darkside had an officially assigned tutor from the Board
of Education, but he rarely met with his tutor for substantive conversation.
Darkside's mother relied on the on-site tutor for this school connection
because she worked long hours in the service industry, and she stated that

> We try to build a lot for this community. We
> We need more people to help for this commun
> lot. . . . We planted seeds over here in this box
> will be beautiful. We picked up the garbage an(
> this fence here. We want to make the grass greer
> and vegetables so that everyone will have enoug\
> that people will have a beautiful environment an(
> done for the community. We try to finish the garde
> our ability before the summertime comes. I did a lo
> mostly with the fence back here, and with planting t
> with the cleanup. So, I did a little bit too.

Darkside's final statement veered from his original scr
to extemporaneously provide added description of his invo
its impact on the overall project. After 6 minutes of this unp\
mentary, Tanda interrupted Darkside by asking, "Darkside, a\
yet?" Tanda's questioning tone seemed to be playful, and she
head back and forth in a way that seemed to say, "Enough, alre,
question was directed toward the camera rather than Darkside
suggesting that although she wanted to remind him that she a\
still needed their opportunities to speak, she also wanted to sh
viewing audience that if given the opportunity, Darkside can a\
speak at length on his views about the importance of science in h\
the community. Darkside finished his statement quickly in respor
Tanda.

After his two coproducers presented their final thoughts, Dark\
volunteered to give the final word. Standing again in the middle of
garden, Darkside spoke passionately about the role and importance
doing science for the community. With increasing intensity and arms wa\
ing in the air, Darkside raised two points: that involvement in a scienc\
project for the community required the involvement of many different
people if it were to be the best science possible, and that science projects in
the community were important ways to make a difference in the community because they made it better than before:

> We are going to have to change this garden to make it the best. We
> have to get a group of people to help us. Our group will do it. We
> will make a difference, make it better than before. We will make it
> into a beautiful community. A better community. A better environ-
> ment, like it was before.

she had little financial or emotional support that would allow her to meet weekly with her son's teachers. Even though he found it "boring," Darkside said that he did not mind this arrangement, because it was better than having to go to school, where his broken leg made him feel unsafe.

As described in Chapter 1, the shelter where Darkside lived offered many education activities for the residents, but also required residents to abide by many rules. Darkside believed that these rules, along with the physical attributes of the shelter (e.g., fences), made it "feel like you on lockdown." In fact, the three things about living at the shelter that Darkside liked least were the security guards, the curfews, and the prisonlike feel. However, along with many of the other youth at the shelter, Darkside believed that following rules was better "than having your head in the street."

The process of locating and keeping space at the shelter was riddled with bureaucratic red tape and games of chance for Darkside and his family. In the transcript segment that follows, Darkside describes these games of chance and the dehumanizing process his family endured in their struggle to gain access to the city shelter system:

> When I was in the seventh grade, my father paid the rent, but the landlord didn't take rent. He said the check was bad. But he didn't give us any warning. Instead the sheriff came to our apartment in the middle of the night. He told us we had 24 hours to vacate the apartment. That is when they also told us the check was bad. We didn't have anywhere to go. My mother and father took us to the EAU [Emergency Assistance Unit]. The EAU, they put us in a smelly, dirty, rotten place where we stayed for 10 days. After that they deemed us ineligible, reason being that my parents only have a "common law marriage." What I mean by that is they were never married by law. They lived together for 15 years. They had three children together, but they was never married by the law. My parents applied again at the EAU for housing. This time we stayed another 10 days at the same rotten place before they told us we were ineligible. My parents, they got some money and paid to get married. They went to the EAU and they put us in a shelter. I never went to school during that time, until we got into a shelter. I never really made such an understanding, but I can see now that my grades were bottom in the seventh grade.

Darkside was quite sophisticated in his analysis of the eligibility process. He made careful distinctions between the process as it played out through city regulations and the people who were left to enact those policies. He knew "it ain't folks like Ula or Jake [the counselors] who makin' them decisions about eligibility." He knew "they care[d]" about him, and believed they were just following the rules. Darkside and Mace, a 10-year-old African American resident, further described the games of chance faced in maintaining shelter space *once it was acquired*:

> DARKSIDE: What are some words that you use to describe living in a homeless shelter?
>
> MACE: Some words that I describe living in a homeless shelter is um (*pause*) some security may say you not eligible, is discharged. Discharged in here is a big word, cause *that's like your life right there when you get discharged from the shelter* (*emphasis added*). Have to start all over, go back to the EAU to sleep in the hard benches. But I'm sayin', here, here, I mean it's all right, but I wouldn't wanna be here. But it's all good, better than nothin'. Better than sleeping out in the cold.
>
> DARKSIDE: Yes, that's true. At least you got a roof over your head, right Mr. Mace?
>
> MACE: Yes, you have a roof overhead, not just that. You could say—you don't even have to be poor. You could just be going through some rough times—
>
> DARKSIDE: Through changes—
>
> MACE: Through changes, once you get on your feet.
>
> DARKSIDE: Get back on your—
>
> MACE: Discharge from the shelter is a very—
>
> DARKSIDE: Big word—
>
> MACE: Important word.

Thus, Darkside believed that living in a homeless shelter was demeaning, even though he was appreciative of having the space. He understood that poverty has complex manifestations and that those manifestations are subject to change.

Missing school and moving around shelters represented only one set of issues Darkside faced in his quest to succeed in school. Although he was generally upbeat about the role of education in his life, he was critical of teachers he believed did not respect his capacity to succeed:

> I mean that the teacher I have, she teaches us nothing. She gives us these worksheets that don't teach us nothing. She don't care what we learn. I think she's dumbing us down, so we won't be smarter than her. . . . She's dumbing us down. She don't want us to be smarter than her. It may be she don't know enough to teach us, but

- Designing and revising models

    Blueprints
    Three-dimensional models

- Planting and building

Darkside participated in almost all these activities as least as far as planning them, although his full-length cast prevented extensive physical participation in actual activities. The main adult teacher in the program initially viewed Darkside's participation as peripheral because he couldn't help out with the physical labor for a crucial 3-month period. Although Darkside faithfully attended the planning meetings, many of the details of the plans were revised and more fully developed while the youth actually worked in the lot. Darkside, however, viewed his participation as central. He described himself as being "very involved" in the project. He noted that his major contributions, especially during the time when he had a full-length cast, were his "ideas" and his "abilities to get other youth involved" in the project—by encouraging them to attend the meetings, by helping them to articulate their ideas for the project, or by persuading them to become more personally invested in the project.

When the main teacher for the after-school program and I compared notes on Darkside, we were both surprised to learn of the differences between how Darkside viewed his participation in the project, and how his participation was viewed by the teacher. We agreed that this difference highlighted even more the power of the roles Darkside played in this project. Indeed, as Darkside described, from the very beginning, he viewed his work in the action research project as important and central to making a difference in the community through beautification: "You want to change the environment and make a difference. That is what we are trying to do to this lot over here"; and "It is important to do things for your community, to make it a better place. That's what we are doing with the lot. Beautify it. Help people want to be there, to spend time there. We need to help our community."

TRANSFORMATIONS

Transformation and the Harshworld

In one of her earlier pieces, hooks (1984) uses the phrase "the harshworld" to describe the beliefs, policies, and structures that the poor Black family confront on a daily basis, such as school- and community-based policies that describe what academic achievement, good studenting, and community participation looks like or federal legislation on health care, affirmative action, tax policies, and child care. Youth living in urban poverty, like the youth in our research, face the harshworld on a daily basis. For Darkside, the harshworld included being dumbed down in school, being on lockdown, facing the reality that most of his peers wanted to leave the neighborhood when they grew up, and understanding that participation in science has been limited to particular people who act in particular ways.

Using hooks's conceptualization of the harshworld is helpful for understanding youths' practices of science because it helps us to see what and how youth engage in a practice of science that is based in transformation. We see Darkside's story transforming two kinds of spaces in particular: the space of "inner-city neighborhoods," in other words, the physical and sociopolitical community in which he resides and the space of "doing science." Put another way, a practice of science is about transforming the harshworlds of the communities in which youth such as Darkside live and the harshworld of science.

What can we learn from Darkside and his involvement in science at the shelter where he lived? What does his life have to say to our own efforts and commitments to work with youth to learn, use, and produce science? Why is transformation an important construct in youths' practices of science?

As we reflect on what we have witnessed and learned from Darkside, it seems to us that Darkside's engagement in science is about many different things, including finding ways to make the community more beautiful; finding ways to involve greater numbers of people; and expanding the ways in which people, especially those not thought of as scientists (among them drug dealers and homeless people), can participate. What seems particularly compelling in Darkside's story, however, is that undergirding each of these decisions about what kinds of science activities should be done and who should be allowed to participate in them is his urge to transform—to transform his neighborhood, the sociopolitical community that frames life inside and outside his neighborhood, and how he and his peers make decisions around what really counts as science.

Broad Participation as a Mode for Transforming Community

Darkside channeled his efforts in the lot project into *broadening* who could participate and why, challenging what legitimate participation looked like, and passionately making a case for why various activities ought to be included in the project. Perhaps the most obvious way in which Darkside facilitated broadening participation was through his helping to organize

Community Day. Community Day, taking place on a Saturday, was designed by the teens to open up to the larger community the work of transforming the lot. The event was advertised by fliers and involved such work as picking up garbage in the lot; building a new fence around the lot; laying a cement foundation for the sign the youth created for the lot; and planting trees, flowers, and vegetables. Darkside helped to design the fliers advertising Community Day and participated in the actual Community Day activities.

To Darkside, Community Day was important because it allowed "more people" to participate in the project. More people were important to Darkside because "good science" would happen "only if everyone were involved" and "because science was about finding answers to *everyone's* questions and needs."

Darkside worked hard to convince his peers of the importance of becoming involved in the community-based science project. In one particular conversation that took place about the time the youth had just finished picking up and sorting through the trash in the lot, Darkside tried to convince 15-year-old Goldberg that their participation in the after-school action research project made both of them part of their own scientific community. Darkside stated, "I think that when we are making the lot into a garden, then we are part of the scientific community because we using science to make the community better. We are part of science. We contributing." Darkside's point was that where the scientific community resides has implications for who is a part of it and for what one must know or be able to do to become a part of it. Of course, this is a much more informal view of the scientific community than the community of professional scientists might hold for themselves. However, what we see as important is how youth have co-opted this ideal for their own lives. When Goldberg disagreed with Darkside, stating, "Because, we not really part of science. We might be doing something for the community, but that doesn't meant we are part of the scientific community," Darkside quickly and excitedly responded:

> Yah, but if we use science, then we are part of the scientific community. Mr. Goldberg, I'm saying that we know enough science. We use what we know about the environment and plants and pollution to transform the lot. We doing this for the community. No one is telling us what to do, or how to do the garden. So, we are part of the scientific community!

As illustrated by this conversation with Goldberg, inclusivity in doing science was important because it allowed science to be responsive to everyone's needs and because it legitimized the social and political context they brought to doing science. As Darkside further explained in an exchange he had with me:

> Like in the abandoned lot action research project, we were doing science. We were using our hands, our minds, figuring out what we need here, what we need there to make the garden. It's like, we start with the lot, and we have to decide what are we going to do with it? It is full of litter and pollution. It has got needles, trash, and all of that nasty stuff. Then, we talk about it, debate it, and decide what to do. What we did was some research on what we *could* do. What was cheap? What would not have too much upkeep? What would other kids not vandalize? We measured the lot, using math and measuring tapes. Then we made maps and 3-D models of what we wanted to do. In the end, we decided on a community garden. That's doing science.

Another significant contribution in Darkside's efforts to convince his peers was his leadership in the production of *The Urban Atmosphere*. He expressed a desire to make the video about life and science in the inner city by teens for teens because he was interested in a research product that would be useful for other youth. In making *The Urban Atmosphere*, Darkside encouraged participation in the video by teens who were not involved in the lot project. He persuaded the other involved teens that part of the video needed to be filmed in the neighborhood, not just at the shelter. He believed that the youth needed to include scenes from the local grocery store, from fast-food places, and from in the streets. In fact, Darkside was the only teen willing to interview the local merchants for the video. Other teens accompanied him to the local merchants and helped to generate the interview questions as well as ideas on the filming sequence, but they were reluctant to actually conduct an interview.

Transforming Spaces

Broadening participation contributed to the transformation of the physical and the sociopolitical community. On the one hand, Darkside wanted the garden to exist in the space across from the shelter because he wanted people to walk by, to "stop and sit down, and to enjoy what the garden has to offer."

On the other hand, this physical transformation meant more than simply giving others a safe and beautiful place to be. It had implications for how the sociocultural community was transformed. One of Darkside's major motivations for helping to transform the abandoned lot into a garden was his desire to be proud of his community; further, he wanted the garden project to be something that he would be "remembered by." Darkside did not want to leave his community when he became an adult. He spoke passionately about wanting to make his neighborhood a place where people wanted to live—not wanted to leave. He wanted his community to be a place where, upon his completion of high school or college, he could still find meaningful relationships, job opportunities, and places to hang. He also wanted to demonstrate to the rest of the world (especially to those who saw his neighborhood and other such inner-city neighborhoods as ugly, scary places) that his neighborhood was beautiful and was a place where its current residents wanted to live and were proud to live. During one particular conversation between two teenage male peers, Goldberg and Steve, living in the shelter and living elsewhere became the focus of conversation. Others responded. Although all the boys agreed that they did not enjoy living in a homeless shelter, one of the boys insisted that eventually he wanted to leave the inner-city community altogether. Darkside responded by calling attention to their work at the lot, reminding the other youth that it was their job to be proud of their community, and asking them to contribute to it so that it would be a place where they would want to live and where other people would want to visit. He told them this was important because it was their community and because he did not want to let the world believe that their communities were no good.

Darkside pushed his fellow community members to consider how their visions for the garden and their subsequent actions were critical to revitalizing the neighborhood. He pushed them to consider how they might use their own constructions of science and self to sustain their community and their actions while also transforming the larger communities. Through transforming the lot, involving as many people as he knew how and building community among them, Darkside wanted to have an impact on how his neighborhood was viewed from the inside out and the outside in.

In fact, the video project itself was designed to teach other youth about life and science in the inner city so that they could do a lot project in other communities, too. In his words, he wanted to "help other teens see how you can do something for the community." He cast his net broadly in creating *The Urban Atmosphere*, including both teens who worked on the garden project and those who did not. He wanted to extend his enactment of agency to other youth. Although Darkside felt that the shelter had him on lockdown with all their rules and regulations and that his science teacher at school was trying to dumb him down, he used the garden project to help his peers work around and resist these limiting qualities of his community.

Transforming Science

Science as Content and Process Skills. At one level, the science of the lot project engaged by Darkside reflected the qualities typically used to describe any science-learning setting: content and process skills. A brief analysis of Darkside's and his peers' scientific activity reveals that much of what they experienced matches well with what the authors of the National Science Education Standards claim is important for high school students. As Table 6.1 illustrates, the students involved in the lot project had multiple opportunities to engage in standards-based science education.

Science as a Tool for Change. At another level, "knowing" or "learning" science expanded on content and process to be a tool for change. As a tool for change, knowing or learning science included, in addition to learning content and skills, applying scientific ideas, recasting the purposes and goals of science, broadening the knowledge base and values essential to doing "good" science, and linking the practice of science with the practices of empowerment and solidarity. We describe these four points in an interconnected fashion below.

Darkside and his peers applied the tools of science to document, critically analyze, plan for, and change the kinds of things in their community that were oppressive to life there. Science was used to determine why the abandoned lot was a danger in the community (the kinds of trash found there, the kinds of infestations that sanitary negligence might facilitate). The evidence gathered through scientific study was then used as a means for arguing to the community and to potential funding sources why they ought to support a project to transform the lot into a garden and to later plan for the garden.

Applying science in this way meant that youth such as Darkside and their families and community members had a say in what ideas were worth exploring, what it meant for exploration to be useful and worthwhile, and what the final outcomes of any explorations ought to be. For example, if we return to Darkside's experiences, we can see how his efforts to transform the physical and sociopolitical community with his peers challenged the reasons for why the doing of science should take place in the community setting. Darkside advocated an action component within science—more important to the process of science than just learning something new about the world is how that knowledge actively gets positioned within everyday practice. Darkside described the project as about doing science for "ourselves" in urban settings. Doing science in urban settings for ourselves was important to him because it enabled him to act on his own needs as well as identified him as an individual who knows *how* to act on his own

Table 6.1. Science Standards and the Lot Project

National Science Education Standard, Grades 9–12: Science as Inquiry	Darkside's and His Peers' Accomplishments
A. Identify questions and concepts that guide scientific investigations	Youth generated issues and related research questions regarding how to make life better for themselves and their peers. They refined their questions so that they were manageable and able to be explored on a teenage level and with minimal resources. The youth settled on transforming the lot into a garden with flowers and vegetables, benches, a stage, and a mural because they desired to make their neighborhood more beautiful, safer, and more presentable to outsiders. They also wanted to learn more about plants and design.
B. Design and conduct scientific investigations	Students evaluated the state of the lot (kinds, quantities, and location of trash, living plants and animals, fence, soil, surrounding buildings). They used their evaluation to determine what kinds of cleanup activities were necessary. They researched the resources necessary for such cleanup activities. They also determined what kinds of plants they wanted and what kinds the garden could support. They researched what it would take to fix the fence and to paint a sign for their lot. They generated a work plan to accomplish these tasks.
C. Use technology and mathematics to improve investigations and communications	Youth measured the dimensions of the lot and the kinds of things contained in and around the lot (fence, wall of adjacent building, etc.), including such properties as perimeter and area, and used these calculations to determine what they would need in their cleanup and transformation efforts.
D. Formulate and revise scientific explanations and models using logic and evidence, and recognize and analyze alternative explanations and models	In the process of generating plans for the lot, the youth researched multiple ideas. They developed multiple plans (based on their ideas), debated and defended these plans amongst themselves, and built 2- and 3-D models of the most agreed upon plans.
E. Communicate and defend a scientific argument	The youth presented their favorite plans to the larger community. They advertised their presentation through fliers, signs, and word of mouth. Through the presentations the youth elicited feedback from the larger community.
F. Understandings about scientific inquiry	Youth learned through experience how all the processes listed in Standards A through E were critical to the development of their lot transformation project.

needs in positive and productive ways. Thus, the purposes and goals of
science were about asking, answering, and acting upon questions to bring
justice to a neighborhood that was largely ignored. Darkside's efforts were
supported in his stance by an after-school science teacher who believed in
youth's abilities to use science as a tool for change. He was also supported
by his peers, who, like him, were willing to use science to make a difference in their community.

Darkside advocated a stance on what good science looked like. According to Darkside, if someone or some group were to enter Darkside's
community to transform the lot, that would be science, but to be *good* science, that individual or group would need to engage in such a process in
collaboration with those who lived in the community. He believed that this
would radically alter the focus and scope of the science to be done. For
example, he described how their community's efforts to improve the lot
would be significantly better and more important than any city program
to improve the lot because the city would not understand their needs. Thus,
for Darkside, participation in the science program was ultimately about
doing good for the self and for others:

ANGIE: But one thing I never thought about before is how you talk
about the science community and doing science as doing
something that you can be proud of and remembered by. I
never thought of those qualities as being part of science or a
requirement of science.
DARKSIDE: Maybe it is not a part of science. Maybe it is just a part
of *doing* science. I'm doing science for my community.
ANGIE: So, the object of doing science is as much to figure
something out for someone, like how the world works or
something, as it is actually producing something useful to be
remembered by? So, science has two parts?
DARKSIDE: There is another part, and that is that it has to be good
for the community. Like with the lot, we are beautifying the
community.

Thus, central to Darkside's idea about doing science for good is the
very idea of doing or acting for the community. In his words, science, and
in particular science in the community, required the following three qualities: "It is something that you do in your community that you can be proud
of. It is something that you do in your community to be remembered by.
And, science is something that will help to beautify and change your community to make it a better place for yourself, your family, and your com-

munity." He used this vision to influence other teens on the action research project.

This action-centered vision of science appears important when contrasted with his school science experiences. The teacher he respected most involved the students in exploration and had given him ideas for experiments to do at home. Those experiences he spoke most negatively about involved dumbing down the curriculum and boring assignments meant to keep students "in their place." Through his talk and action in the action research project this is just what Darkside attempted to avoid. Darkside believed that science was important for him to learn. He had signed up for science in school because he believed it would help him get a job and to go to college. Although he believed that he learned some science in his science class, he did not see learning science in schools as making him part of the scientific community or connecting him to his own community.

Darkside's intentions, actions, and descriptions of his actions call into question connections between position, power, and knowledge. Here, Darkside's knowledge is experientially based; it is a representation of his reality and he uses his experience as lens to understand, critique, and transform the realities of his local community. In the process, he also transforms science and his place in science.

LOOKING AHEAD

It seems to us that as an urban homeless youth, Darkside lived in the borderland and used his personal experiences there to build an agenda for understanding and transforming the world around him. Without his passionate intervention on the courtyard or in the computer room, it is not clear that the other youth would have persevered, especially during the times when their efforts were vandalized by outsiders who continued to litter the lot even after the cleanup. Certainly, without his interventions we would not have understood the power, resistance, and solidarity embedded in the lot project. Yes, we believe we would have understood the power embedded in youth working to transform an abandoned lot, but we would not have understood this action in terms of building community, transforming outsiders' views of his neighborhood, or something to be remembered by. We would not have seen the intersections between Darkside's practice of science and the histories of oppression, anger, hope, and home that Darkside made so visible. Darkside and his peers remind us that we need to work to see how youth try to communicate a broader vision of science from their borderlands on a daily basis.

Recent research in science education urges us to consider culture, language, and daily experience as a basis for constructing more inclusive and more empowering science education for youth. Fundamental to these studies is the claim that science itself is a cultural construct and that science educators ought to be open to how youth construct science in our presence in classrooms and other informal learning sites. My work with Darkside, and other youth, however, suggests that understanding science as a cultural practice, although important, is not enough. If we can also begin to learn how to see the science in the work that youth do and to see the youth as scientific in their efforts, then we may begin to see how youths' lives transform how we understand the nature and practice of science and the role of science in the lives of urban youth. Darkside certainly had a broad field of resources that he drew on to craft his own practices of science, and he used his cultural location and power among his peer group to help ensure that those resources were valued.

Darkside's practice of science as displayed in the lot transformation project urges us to consider why it might be important to think about science not only as a way of understanding the world but also as a political activity. By *political activity* we mean that the doing of science is framed around power, status, and influence in its history, practice, and implications. Darkside shows us that the science the youth did and the knowledge that resulted from such practice is crafted through personal experience, imprinted with the values, beliefs, and assumptions of its creators. The implications of such a stance are that science (and any education in science) will only be equitable and empowering if students learn—in addition to the standard knowledge base of ideas and skills—to uncloak those assumptions, to draw strength from their exposure, and to expand understandings of the agreed-upon boundaries for where and how scientific ideas are generated.

Understanding science as a political activity is not devoid of content. Adequate access to this core of knowledge facilitates academic success and helps to give authority and insight into issues such as environmental racism or facilitate medical decisions such as those involved in recruitment to high-risk pharmaceutical clinical trials. In the lot project, youth needed to learn about the local geology and climate in order to plan for a garden. They had to understand different forms of urban pollution and its impact on soil quality and plant growth. They needed skills in mathematics and literacy to gather, analyze, and share useful data. However, Darkside's story suggests that access to scientific ideas is only the beginning. Youth need opportunities to apply scientific ideas in their lives; to understand how doing science is intimately connected to larger social, cultural, and political issues; and to value the ways in which their own personal and community stories contribute to how, why, and when science is done.

to maintain certain values, priorities, and ways of being together. Drawing primarily from the experiences and interviews of the young people at Southside Shelter, most, but not all, of whom worked on the lot renovation project partly described in Chapter 6, we present a vision for the kind of community the youth believe is important in supporting their science practices.

COMMUNITY AND SCIENCE AMONG HOMELESS YOUTH

In what follows, we share two detailed snapshots of youth doing science: "Doing REAL Science: A View From the Inside" and "Doing REAL Science: A View from the Margin, but Not Marginal."

Doing REAL Science: A View From the Inside

In the fall of 1998, we worked with teens at Southside Shelter to create a student-centered, community-based science project.[1] During the first week with the teenagers, Dana, the main teacher, began by engaging the youth in group conversation around questions such as, What are the concerns of young people today? The youth described teen pregnancy, being shot or making it to the next day, AIDS, unprotected sex, gangs, alcohol use, and adults' perceptions of youth, described as negative especially if you're Black.

Dana helped the teens focus on those concerns they cared most about and believed they could do something about. At first, the youth were focused on "raising money" and giving to charity as a way to bring about positive change. As Dana talked with them about why charities were important to them, one teen stated his opinion that, as homeless kids, "we are charity." The consensus that they were charity marked them as "the end of the line" and made more urgent the notion that if they wanted to make changes in their community, they might have to begin to do so themselves.

Dana had the youth refocus their attention by designing murals, writing raps, and role-playing their concerns. One concern that emerged was that of an abandoned lot across the street from the shelter. Mainly, the youth were concerned that the lot housed drug deals, and was generally an "unsafe" place to be. In talking about the lot, the youth realized that though they may not be able to do something about the actual drugs or drug paraphernalia that got passed through the lot, and though they may not be able to protect themselves from the gangs who threw bottles into the lot, they could at least try to improve the lot so that eventually it might not be the kind of place that drug users or gangs wanted to exploit. Furthermore, the lot was definitely an eyesore. It was abandoned and full of garbage, including sharp and dangerous objects. A chain-link fence that had sharp fragments protruding in several places surrounded the lot.

The youth decided that one thing they could do was clean up the lot and turn it into a usable community space. A community space would be clean and inviting and would deter criminal activity because the space would no longer be abandoned. Dana led the students through brainstorming possibilities for the empty lot. Ideas included a basketball court, swimming pool, arcade, playground, sandbox, garden, stage, cybergames, laser challenge, and a penny store. She had the youth conduct a site assessment to determine the feasibility of their ideas. Was the space large enough to house all these suggestions? What existed in the lot currently and what was its history? Was the soil viable for planting?

The process of converting the lot into a usable community space consisted of four major steps.[2] First, the youth articulated their desires and needs and set a plan in place to map out an action research project that would affect their lives in a positive way. The young people evaluated the conditions of the lot and reported their findings to the group in order to refine their vision for the lot. In teams, they measured the space, recorded its contents (living and nonliving things), took photographs, and drew diagrams of the present condition of the space. Each team, although pursuing the collective motive of documenting the lot qualities, also had an individual own motive that framed its work. Some teams were more interested in the possibility of building a stage and painting a mural on the building that was adjacent to the lot, while other teams were more interested in a playground. Some members of some teams did not really know, or yet care, what would or should happen to the lot. Student reports and drawings ranged from one-page pencil-on-paper sketches of possible designs to elaborate presentations of what kind of litter existed in the lot and the feasibility of preparing the lot for future use. Each group answered questions and defended the practicality of its idea with information gathered in the lot assessment. The shared evaluation winnowed out items from the list, for the findings showed ways in which some of the ideas were not realistic or somehow did not fit the space and its qualities properly; for example, cybergames and laser challenge were dropped, and based on the findings of the site measurement, the lot was judged too small for a basketball court. Eventually, the youth's ideas were ultimately funneled into one larger idea: a multipurpose community garden. The garden would contain fruits and vegetables to be tended, harvested, and sold by the teens. However, it would also house a stage for community performances and a mural depicting the worlds of the youth who built the garden.

In the second step the young people researched their topic and engaged in major design efforts. The youth prepared conceptual drawings and models and shared their efforts with the neighborhood community. In addition to the drawings and model-building, part of this process included book and Internet research on community gardens and on what kinds of plants survive in the geographical region of the lot. Also included were conversations with professionals, visits to local gardens, and examination of pictures of other community gardens and structures, such as trellises and storage sheds. The teens worked on various structures, planning the layout of the design and the materials they would need (a process modeled by the landscape designer). The process continued for several sessions, each time youth adding or revising from where others left off. The number of structures included in the design plan increased steadily from the initial drawings in October to the conceptual drawings in January to the model in March. One youth's initial drawing, for instance, included a laser park and an arcade. In the later two-dimensional and three-dimensional designs there were trees, a pond, a stage, flowerbeds, garbage cans, and more. This final model was shared and revised at a community meeting for the wider public, at which the youth presented their ideas, distributed fliers with specific information, and answered questions. Prior to the meeting some of the youth were nervous about sharing their ideas with the community. As one youth put it, "Who wants to listen to shelter kids?"

In the third step, the youth applied their research and design to the actual task of the lot renovation. Their activities included clearing the lot; replacing the fence; and planting vegetables, flowers, and trees. They also built pathways and borders to the gardened areas. Some of the major work was accomplished at an event created by the youth: The group had decided that the community needed to be more involved and developed what they called Community Day, an all-day event on a Saturday when the larger community was invited in to help the kids with their lot cleanup and gardening plans. The teens actively publicized the event, distributing fliers to families, staff, local store owners, and neighbors. The days were mainly planned by Dana and the youth, but were tailored by the expertise of those present each Saturday.

In the fourth step, the youth shared their findings with the larger community. Although we label this step as "fourth," temporally it cut across the first three steps. The youth communicated their ideas through the design of the mural, which included pictures of the youth working on the garden and slogans, which represented their thinking about the garden. They also communicated their ideas through what became known as *The Book*, a three-ring binder that kept the history of the group and project and

Tanda participated in the Community Days and found other venues to communicate her ideas.

We list here these informal courtyard chats as a significant form of marginal participation in REAL simply because it is noteworthy that anyone was talking at all about the project in substantive ways. In all our interactions with youth in out of school settings it was not often that we have witnessed impromptu conversations about the content of their science classes.

BUILDING SCIENCE COMMUNITIES IN SUPPORT OF YOUTH LIVES AND PRACTICES OF SCIENCE

These two snapshots of youth's involvement in REAL raised questions for us about participation in a science project or membership in a "science community":

- What does it mean to participate in a science community?
- Who should be allowed to participate in a science community and how should participation be measured?
- How do decisions around who can participate and what participation entails influence the purposes, goals, and outcome of that community?
- How does the form of a community sustain youth's practices of science, especially when those practices sometimes contradict standard practices?

We talked with the youth, including those who directly and indirectly participated in the lot transformation project to learn more about how they believed their community supported them as teenagers, their science activities, and their beliefs about the role and purpose of science in their lives. The majority of the youth interviewed consistently revealed three principal dimensions of the kind of community that supports their science practices: the aim of building a community around "real science," a desire for and the challenge of inclusiveness, and a responsiveness to the urban context. We take up each of these themes below.

Building a Community Around "Real" Science

Doing "real" science was a theme that permeated youth's talk and actions at Southside Shelter. For the youth in this study, real science appeared to be based largely upon three criteria:

- That the science was not fake, meaning that it involved both action and understanding relevant and meaningful to the community engaged in the scientific activity
- That the science activity had import for a community larger that those immediately or directly involved
- That there were structured means for passing on scientific information, ideas, or outcomes to those in the community

The youth's discourse around the lot project reflected their belief that they were members of a community rather than "charity." The group initially called themselves Shelter Boys, even though several girls were participating in the project, and primary identification with the project had been that they were working together on after-school science because they lived together at a shelter. However, as the project progressed, the teens began to debate a new name for the project. When brainstorming a name for the group the youth thought up such names as Designer, Activity, Community, Gardener, Service, Caring, Caring Squad, Agriculture, Helping Hands, and Environmental. From these words, they decided on REAL, or Restoring Environments and Landscapes.

The name REAL signified to an enormous extent how the youth thought of themselves, thought about science, and thought about how these two came together in their neighborhood. It reflected a vision that was inclusive, meaningful, and relevant to the lives of young people. One boy distinguished REAL from school when he said, "I thought it was gonna be like a project, like in school, you know like a fake project."

All the teens involved—whether those most centrally involved in the design and planning or those working from the margins—were members of the REAL community. For example, for Tanda, the name REAL signified the very reasons that the teens worked together on the project: science was about real life, and building a safe garden for the children in the neighborhood fit that ideal. She stated that science was "the things you have to do in your life to survive" such as "taking care of babies" and "finding ways to get out [of the shelter]."

Tanda challenged the rules for participation in the after-school science program, encouraging us to create multiple avenues for participation in REAL. Kobe argued with his peers to justify the importance of the lot project, especially in light of the continuing violence and vandalism that he believed likely to happen in the renovated lot. Darkside pushed his peers to consider how their visions for life in the inner city, which included their visions for the lot transformation, were critical to revitalizing their neighborhood.

Little provided a similar perspective in her commentary about a local eatery also filmed for *The Urban Atmosphere*:

We eat the food from here. We need to find out what kind of shit they put in that food. It's not good for you. I heard that they closed down for sanitation. People getting sick there. We got to find out what we eat. They killin' us.

Later, she pointed out that studying the eatery and its cleanliness were the kinds of things the young people should do as an after-school science community. She believed that this kind of science was just as real as REAL. She later stated that she believed that both school science and after-school science were important to her life: School science was important because it might help you to "go to college or get a job" (and Little wanted to become a pediatrician) but working with other kids to make a video was also important because it helped with "life."

Another aspect of real science supported by the youth community focused on *how* and *why* ideas were shared. Many of the teens talked about the importance of sharing the products created by their peer group. For example, Yolanda described her role in their REAL science community as "making the lot better for [her] children," so that they will have a "place to play." This was also the case for Darkside: "It is something that you do in your community that you can be proud of. It is something that you do in your community to be remembered by. And, science is something that will help to beautify and change your community to make it a better place." For Darkside, the idea of passing on knowledge and products was tied to being proud of what it was he was passing down. Several students described the importance of sharing ideas from their generation with the next generation by involving and teaching the children about how to care for their environment.

Thus, the youth wanted to be part of a community that would support real science. For the youth in our study, this meant that their REAL science community should engage in a science that is useful; that the science that they do should have some goal that will make a difference in their lives or at least have meaning in their lives; and that the outcomes of their science practices ought to affect more than just them, the creators of the science.

A Desire for and the Challenges of Inclusiveness

The two snapshots of the youth's participation in REAL also bring to the fore the element of inclusion: What individuals, locations, and events ought to be included in youth's science activities and why? What repercussions does *who participates* or *where participation is allowed* have on the outcomes of the project? For example, Tanda openly raised questions about whose ideas were listened to in the lot project. She made claims about how everyone needed to work on the project or it would not benefit anyone. Along with Darkside, she purposefully sought out students not involved in the lot project to be interviewed in *The Urban Atmosphere* to broaden the level of people involved. As these two snapshots suggest, inclusion played out in the youth's descriptions primarily in two ways:

- Who should be included (interage participation, open-mindedness towards how people contribute as well as towards an individual's personal problems, a greater interest in getting the work of the community done than following the rules)
- The requirements of inclusiveness (being committed, responsible, and responsive)

Who Should be Included? Who should be included in the youth's science events was an issue that emerged in the youth's conversations around REAL over and over again. Like Tanda's ideas regarding the need to listen to everyone's ideas, the other youth's responses consistently revealed that "all" people should have the opportunity to be included in any community-based science project. Including all people meant including a wide range of people who lived and worked around the neighborhood where the science event occurred. Real science required the participation of everyone. Shorty, a 14-year-old African American girl expressed the view that including as many people as possible in their science community was important even if that meant including people who were normally marginal to the community. When Darkside asked Shorty if "drug dealers or dope addicts" should be part of their science community, Shorty stated, "If they want to make a difference in the community with the kids, like help them with like fixing the lot up and stuff, yea." Darkside pushed Shorty even further in her explanation:

DARKSIDE: What happens if a man, what happens if a man give us, do our commercial about this lot right here and people lookin' at it? A thousand people lookin' at this commercial and they want to get interested? They want to, can they join in that community, in this community?
SHORTY: Yea. Cause it's also part of they community too.
DARKSIDE: It would make all the people get up and help.
SHORTY: Yea.
DARKSIDE: *This is what I like about science!*

Including all people also meant that the youth possessed the authority to be members of a science community. For example, Darkside stated that his work helping to renovate the abandoned lot into something usable made him a "part of the scientific community of [his neighborhood]." He explained that the kids involved in the lot project were members of their own scientific community even though their work might not be as expensive or fancy as that of scientists.

Youth placed boundaries around "who should count in the all" that are also worth considering. According to the teens, being a member of a science community was not an unmitigated right. Being included carried with it responsibility and commitment, or as Mace, a 10-year-old described it: "Oh, what you got to do to stay a member of your community is you can't do drugs, you have to support your community, and you got to be there when stuff go down in your community, you know? You gotta always be around." More than half the youth believed that most people should be involved if they participated in ways that were helpful to that community.

Part of being committed was also about giving the time necessary to make the community work. According to Sting, a 10-year-old boy, "To be a member of a community meant helping out, taking time out to build the community to make it stronger, 'cause first you have to have a foundation. And for y'all stupid people out there that don't know what a foundation is, a foundation is, a foundation is the bottom." Tanda further exemplified this point with her unit and courtyard chats.

In one particular conversation, Darkside argued with Goldberg in an attempt to convince him that his participation in REAL made him part of the REAL scientific community. He stated, "I think that when we are making the lot into a garden, then we are part of the scientific community because we using science to make the community better. We are part of science. We contributing." Darkside's point was that where the scientific community resided had implications for who was a part of the community and what one must know or be able to do to become a part of the community.

As discussed in Chapter 6, although Darkside's perspective of how the teens were a part of the science community was more extreme than that of his peers, all but two of the youth believed all should have the opportunity to participate. Shorty's statement about the drug dealers reflected the belief that even those individuals who were part of the neighborhood, but who did not fit social norms, ought to be considered for inclusion as long as they contributed to the community. One's location in the neighborhood where the project took place gave one the right to be part of one's own REAL science community. This concept gave the youth authority to claim not only who should participate but also what the community is or should be about.

Inclusiveness Requires Responsiveness and Respect. Questions around who should participate were centered on the youth's desire to be respected by their peers and to have their needs responded to. According to several of the teens, "good" science was responsive to all people's needs and therefore required the input of all. For instance, Tanda described how everyone needed to be involved or it "don't benefit no one." Being respected by adults was an issue that came up several times in our conversations with Little, especially around the efforts of REAL. At one point, she felt that the young people were capable of accomplishing a great deal with the project but were not respected by the adults for their efforts:

> Yes, because most . . . mostly in here is mostly kids and that's all you usually see around here. . . . a lot of grownups think, a lot of adults think that children can't do a lot of stuff, which is not true. Children could do the same things that adults could do. We might not get paid for it, but at least we'll help!

These ideas are in contrast to the youth's experiences as homeless youth, where decisions about housing, schooling, and social services are usually made without family consultation. Many of the youth agreed with Darkside that everyone should be part of the REAL science community because science was about finding answers to their questions and needs. Although not all the youth articulated the belief that good science required input from all, the overwhelming majority of the teens did specify that if their ideas were not included they would not feel respected and the outcomes of the lot project would be unsatisfactory.

The notion of responsiveness played out in two ways for the teens: in how they envisioned leadership, and in how they supported one another in "nonstandard" practices. Youth valued leadership that was inclusive and responsive. Several of the teens described how membership in a community could be suffocating if the community was maintained hierarchically. Although leaders were important, according to the youth, they should be allowed to emerge naturally among the teens and should rotate based on who had a "good idea" for a particular need to be met. Steve and Goldberg described how leadership decisions ought to rotate based on who had a "good idea at the time."

This aspect of community seemed to be particularly important, given that every one of the teens we interacted with at Southside (and Hope) described negative experiences with hierarchically managed "shelter communities" and "school communities." For example, all the youth described the homeless shelter community where they lived through the language of rules, regulations, and punishments. In the transcript segment that follows, Little describes a set of negative experiences with the regulations structure at the shelter:

DARKSIDE: And what happens if you don't follow rules and
    regulations [at the shelter]?
LITTLE: Um, you get a warning, when you get signed up . . . signed
    in and signed out in red. Um, they discharge you or, they send
    you to another shelter.
DARKSIDE: None of 'em ever treat you mean?
LITTLE: They treat you like, like if you a piece of trash. They'll call
    the cops on you. They try to do something to make your case
    get closed in welfare or something like that.

Similar to Little, other youth described how the hierarchical leadership structure at the shelter made them feel as if they were "locked in a cage," "in prison," or "like babies." These kinds of hierarchical communities the youth experienced at the shelter appeared to further alienate the youth from where they lived and served as a constant reminder of their status as homeless individuals.

A desire to be part of a community that valued and supported youth and their efforts to go against "standard practice" was also involved in youth's requirement for inclusion. Many of the young people we have written about in this text have broken rules, written and unwritten, with the support of their peers in order to have their lives reflect the kinds of autonomy and freedom usually granted to other youth of their age. In previous chapters we described how Junior bent the rules of community service so that he could participate in the science events of building bird feeders and making ice cream. We wrote about how Tanda bent the rules around participation in after-school science at Southside Shelter in order to participate in REAL. We described how the children at Hope Shelter used the after-school science program as a legitimate place to have pets at the shelter—a direct violation of normal shelter policy.

Several of the youth talked about wanting to be part of a community in after-school science that would give them a chance to help improve their neighborhood. Teenagers, and particularly inner-city teenagers, are often erroneously labeled as youth who don't care about anything but themselves and their immediate futures. This was not the case for the youth in this study. They needed a supportive venue, however, to express what they cared about as well as an opportunity to demonstrate how their caring connected to a broader vision for society. For example, Darkside wanted to work against the prevailing social norms that defined his neighborhood as not a good place in which to live or grow up. Unfazed by messages he heard in the media, he did not want to leave his neighborhood when he grew up. He agreed that it might be a dangerous place filled with eyesores such as the abandoned lot. However, he believed that it was his and his neighbors responsibility to improve the neighborhood and to help others see the beauty in his neighborhood. Indeed, this was his primary motivation for participating in REAL and for leading the effort to produce *The Urban Atmosphere*.

Kobe, as we described in Chapter 2, was a leading gang member and had talked with us about his life goals and aspirations in only nonacademic terms. Yet through his participation in REAL, he had a safe place to try out a science identity. This is a significant point. Kobe was widely popular in a peer group that openly resisted schooling and standard measures of success. To participate in science and then to later claim to want science as a backup career is a powerful example of the kind of nonstandard support he received from his peers.

Thus, inclusiveness involved interage participation, open-mindedness toward how people contribute as well as toward an individual's personal problems, and a greater interest in getting the work of the community done than that involved in merely following the rules. Inclusiveness relied on being committed, responsible, and responsive.

Responsiveness to the Urban Context

The young people reported that they wanted to be part of a community that was responsive to the urban context. According to the youth, responsiveness to the urban context was important because of the ways in which urban settings brought together people, nature, and technologies. Many of the youth described urban life as about "no privacy" and "everybody [knowing] what is going on with everyone else." Many of the youth described the importance of the large number of people living close together, and the many and different kinds of buildings, subways, bridges, tunnels, and other structures that marked and separated different parts of cities.

In the transcript segment that follows, Darkside asked Shorty about the differences she perceived between the urban community and the suburban community. When Shorty initially suggested that she had "no idea," Darkside answered his own question by prompting Shorty to think about how personal knowledge and experience was public domain in urban settings but not necessarily so in suburban settings. Shorty followed Darkside's lead by adding examples about how urban settings facilitate the public sharing of knowledge:

> DARKSIDE: I'm gonna talk about this one. What is the difference between an urban scientific community and a suburb scientific community?
> SHORTY: I have no idea.

DARKSIDE: There is a difference. You know if you live in the
    suburbs, you know people mind they business or so. In a city
    everybody gets involved, do s———.
SHORTY: Oh that's what you talkin' about?
DARKSIDE: Yea.
SHORTY: Yea, it's a difference.
DARKSIDE: Could you explain?
SHORTY: Like, OK like if you live in a city, and there's a fight,
    everybody probably gonna wind up knowin' or a accident,
    everybody would know 'cause it's gonna be in the news.
DARKSIDE: Yes.
SHORTY: And the other one, everybody stays to themselves.
DARKSIDE: Everybody mind they own business. Everybody do they
    own thing, mind they own business.

Darkside developed this question on his own. When one of us later
asked him why he felt this was an important question to ask the other youth,
he explained that "urban" is different from most places because of the
"people" and the "buildings," and that this difference has an impact on
the REAL science community.

In a conversation one of us had with Goldberg and his sister, Mia, we
used Darkside's questions about urban versus suburban and posed it to
these two young people. Both Goldberg and Mia agreed that suburban
people "do their own thing," have their own cars, and use them alone to
go and do whatever they want. They also explained that in the city, and in
particular in the inner city, many people do not have cars. City people have
to work and play with other people around, and that leads city people to
make "better relations with other people." They used this explanation to
suggest that these different kinds of circumstances make them different
from suburban youth and make their REAL science community different
too. Mia stated that a suburban science community might "involve less
people" and that it might be "less real." They used the case of the abandoned lot they were working on as their example: A suburb might "not
allow a trashed abandoned lot to exist," and the "suburb would clean it
up itself." Even if the youth cleaned up the lot in a suburb, it was not because they needed to in order to make their neighborhood better, as was
their own current circumstance; it was because they were asked to join a
volunteer activity. This is supported by the young people's decision to call
their lot renovation project REAL.

As Mia's statement reflects, it was not so much that the teens saw their
community as different because it was urban as it was that this difference
was essential to the productivity and the reality of the community. Accord-

ing to Jolanda, a 16-year-old Latina, "The bad way of all these buildings make us deal with certain things even if we don't want to." Thus the urban nature of the youth's community also seemed to be an important marker for the kind of REAL science community they believed supported their science practices and their lives. Elements such as buildings and other technological structures such as highways; the people; and the interactions between buildings, other structures, and people influence the different needs that a scientific community might respond to, and the ways in which the scientific community uniquely connects to their lives.

COMMUNITY, SCIENCE EDUCATION, AND URBAN YOUTH

What does the youth's participation in REAL tell us about the role and importance of community in their efforts to build a practice of science? How do these ideas stack up against efforts to reform science education?

We know from the literature in urban education that the communities that youth belong to are important to youth and their well-being. Youth feel more important and experience less despair when involved in communities that value and respect their backgrounds and contributions, especially when their backgrounds and experiences deviate from that which has been traditionally valued (Battistich, Solomon, Kim, Watson, & Schaps, 1995). Their success is, in part, attained by learning to "fit" within a community, which includes the ability to learn the discursive practices and norms of behavior. For example, Farrell (1991) describes how urban high school dropouts label themselves as "inadequate" members of their school community when they have failed their coursework, even when that failure was the result of cultural incongruence between the teachers or the curriculum and the students rather than an artifact of their intelligence. Fordham (1996) illustrates how some students outside the culture of power in schools resisted schooling processes and expectations forming their own counter and more supportive communities of resistance such as gangs even though these groups are often looked upon less favorably by the larger society.

Further, we know that communities have to be authentic and adhere to their purpose if they are to feel meaningful to youth. The designers of the National Science Education Standards argue that more "authentic" and "inquiry-based" science classes help students to develop greater connections to science and to the scientific community. It has also been argued that science learning happens at deeper and more meaningful levels when students engage in the kinds of practices and community norms modeled by the scientific community (Duschl, 1990). The Standards also tell us that strong science learning communities have strong external connections (NRC, 1996). The local community is composed of many specialists, including those in transportation, healthcare delivery, communications, computer technologies, music, art, cooking, mechanics, and many other fields that have scientific aspects. In addition, strong links between the science-learning community and the larger social community are necessary for all citizens to engage in scientific and technological debate.

In many ways the youth's views on community correlate well with those put forth by the reform-based literature in science education. The youth make a case for including as many people as possible for authenticity in their science work and for a responsibility both to the science at hand and to the members of the community. However, if we peel away the layers regarding membership in and purposes for participation in this community, stark differences emerge. The three themes reported in this chapter (real science, inclusiveness, and the urban context) suggest to us that two additional concerns ought to be addressed in developing the construct of community—implications for where science ought to happen with and for youth, and why and what science gets done among youth.

The Question of Where

As the youth at Southside Shelter eloquently described, they have their own scientific community that exists in their neighborhood. Squarely positioning "their own scientific community" in their neighborhood is not a trivial idea to the youth. It is where they live, where their questions come from, and what they have to deal with on a day-to-day basis. Of course the youth have interests that extend beyond their neighborhood and that are of interest to many teens in many locations. However, when the idea of a local scientific community is applied to school science it raises questions about how we perceive and use local resources dynamically in building learning communities that support youth's efforts to engage in the meaningful practice of science. In most reform-based literature the local community is important for both its human component and its physical/material component. However, the aims of integrating these resources are more geared toward standard science learning than helping youth develop and refine their own science practices, although there are some notable exceptions (see Bouillion & Gomez, 2001; Hammond, 2001; Rahm, 2002; Seiler, 2001).

In addition to the human, physical, or material components of location is the *political* aspect of location. Our identification of how youth co-opt science was meant to capture the idea that youth were critical of what went on in their lives and in their neighborhoods, and that they created a practice of science to act on their critical understandings. It makes sense then that on the one hand the young people wanted to be inclusive of everyone in their REAL science community, for this speaks to the ways in which they have felt excluded in school, in society, and at the shelters. On the other hand, while the young people described a desire to include "all" in their science communities, they delineated particular boundaries and expectations for those who were ultimately to be included: they had to be around when things went down, they had to be committed to the members of the community and to the neighborhood where the work transpired, they had to be willing to share leadership and to be respectful of others' ideas, and they had to be willing to look past standard social norms if the level of contribution was to be worthwhile.

The Question of What Science Gets Done and Why

The youth in our study have pushed the point about where science is done to make the case that the *where* plays a role in the practice of science they create together. As documented in Chapters 4–6, transformation occurs within several domains, including the physical, social, and scientific. In the building of the picnic table, in Claudia's desk, or in the renovation of the community lot, the youth made changes to their physical world and used those changes to influence a larger group of people. Indeed, the location of the scientific activity and of the community in support of that science activity is connected to the local reasons for what they do and why they do it just as much as it is connected to what kinds of community resources are available.

Furthermore, in contrast to the goals of the national reform initiatives, which urge teachers to work with students to help them feel like members of a scientific community through engaging in the activities of scientists, the youth did not feel as if they were members of a scientific community unless their scientific activities actually contributed to their lives or their neighborhoods. This adds an additional requirement to the suggestions levied by reformers. For these youth, "real" membership depends on doing what scientists do *and* doing so in a way that fundamentally informed their lives. For example, although the youth felt as though they were "contributors" when they worked on community projects, they felt that their practice of science was ultimately a contribution to the community, and not necessarily to science. This distinction is subtle but important—it shifts the emphasis from science for science's sake to science for society's sake, where society at large is in need of its own transformation in order for equity and justice to be promoted, and where all people have power and voice, including those who might not ordinarily be included, such as homeless people.

However, the youth believed that participation ought to be limited to those people who were actively involved in productive and responsive activities regarding the world around them. Members of the local scientific community participate in ways that are helpful, whatever that help tends to look like at that moment. Here science is a tool that helped to frame but did not centralize their existence. It seems to us that reform initiatives, because they are framed within the context of science education, place science in the center of thought and action. Being a member of the scientific community, in these efforts, means helping prod science along. Even when the reform-based literature discusses the importance of all people knowing enough science to engage in public debate around issues of scientific and technological concern, the emphasis is on the problems framed by science rather than the problems framed by life, and in our work, life in poverty.

LOOKING AHEAD

The themes of power and co-opting science spaces, relevant science and activation of resources, and transformations, brought to the fore the importance of how youth reposition themselves as individuals and as members of a community with the power to be autonomous and to change their world. The theme of community connects these previous themes together and gives us a way to understand why and when youth come together to create their own practices of science.

The REAL community's efforts to transform the lot, and Ruben's efforts to lobby his peers and his teachers to make the science project be "furniture for the clubhouse," are obvious examples, but if we look closely we see many other examples. The creation and production of *The Urban Atmosphere*, the building of the grackle bird house, and the insect safari that led to insects as pets all are examples of how youth relied on each other to build a science around their lives and their worlds. What youth want out of a community that supports their practices of science is deeply tied to their visions of science and their beliefs about what they can accomplish in science spaces.

In the United States, current science reform efforts are built on visions of scientists, science, and the scientific community that are myths based on superhuman qualities and insular behaviors (McGinn & Roth, 1999). These visions are not tenable, because scientific agendas are informed by a community that encompasses more than only scientists, and such a vision neglects the day-to-day practice, struggles, and meaning-making of scientists and the situationally contingent understandings and agreements scientists construct. Furthermore, scientific research is influenced by the overall research context and the specific research situation, and the situated ways in which scientists act, think, and work converge with the descriptions of just plain folks (Lave, 1988; Roth & McGinn, 1999). This is where the youth discussed in this book push forward our thinking about science for all. As we seriously integrate the needs of all learners into a science for all, we need to consider the repercussions this has for the construction of community in science classrooms, especially as it relates to the goals and purposes of science and schooling.

CHAPTER 8

Empowering Science Education and Youth's Practices of Science

BUILDING A SOCIALLY JUST WORLD

The stories in this book speak not only to the ways in which power, access to knowledge, equity, social justice, and culture play a role in how youth experience science but also to how youth respond to difficult situations in order to create a practice of science that has power and meaning in their lives. These stories also underscore our core belief that we must understand how science, schooling, and society might intersect in science education settings to help build a more socially just, critically informed, and sustainable society.

Yet the United States has struggled, as a nation, with how to best provide equitable science opportunities in school for youth from high-poverty, urban backgrounds. Should high-poverty schools be given additional resources to help them improve science instruction? Should low-performing schools, which are disproportionately located in high-poverty, urban communities, have funds taken away or be closed down when tests scores demonstrate "failing achievement"?

At the local level, schools in high-poverty, urban districts scramble to meet new state and local standards for science achievement. They are searching for funds with which to buy triple-beam balances and microscopes, in order to foster authentic science investigations but also because they are required to do so by the skills component of high-stakes exams. They are searching for certified teachers and for programs to help those teachers learn about life in urban schools. They are searching for ways to concentrate their attention on mathematics and literacy—the subjects of the key high-stakes exams used in measuring school success—while trying not to diminish the place or importance of other subject areas such as science or social studies, art or music. At the individual level, students are working hard to beat the negative stereotypes placed on them by the media, in popular culture, and by policy makers.

In our own work teaching and researching science education in high-poverty, urban communities, we too have been struggling with similar issues and questions. On the one hand, we are familiar with the material that our professional communities claim is important for students to learn so they may be scientifically literate. And we agree with much of what is written. After all, access to key ideas, skills, and ways of knowing are crucial for understanding and questioning almost every aspect of life in a modern society. We are aware of the power that is conferred by scientific literacy in an individual's and a community's life—from being able to understand or question a doctor's decision to rallying together to fight environmental racism. We also know that high-poverty, urban youth historically have not been well served by schools and often resist historical discrimination by refusing to be placated or drummed.

The solutions to these dilemmas about access and opportunity in science education seem so simple in theory: Create science lessons that are student centered, culturally relevant, and deeply meaningful in terms of the content presented and the lives of those learning that content. Hire certified teachers and offer more laboratory experiences that are both hands-on and minds-on. Offer students opportunities to engage in the culture of science, including learning about the discursive practices of the scientific community, scientific writing, and the habits of mind of scientists.

Yet in our efforts to implement these ideals, we have struggled with the practical realities that they have raised for us. For example, how should we respond to a high school student like Kobe, who says he wants to have science as a "backup career" if sports does not work out, yet who also skips more classes than he attends because of family and gang responsibilities? How do we make our science lessons meaningful for someone like Claudia, who is convinced that her teacher is mean because she does not let them play or who, because of her poverty, cannot bring to class even the simplest home-based supplies for hands-on science activities? Claudia's school is resource strapped, and hands-on activities are sometimes only attainable when students and families help with the supplies. How do we respond to a student like Juan, who demonstrates an amazing intuitive capacity to think through difficult spatial relations problems but who only desires to apply those skills to being a rocklayer, like his father and his grandfather? How do we build and sustain a rigorous student-centered science unit when the students for whom the unit is being designed seem to change their minds about what they are interested in and what matters to them on a day-to-day basis?

We found ourselves struggling daily with the questions that opened this text:

- What concerns do young people living in urban poverty have? How do they understand, articulate, and respond to these concerns? How do these concerns frame their lives?
- How do poor, urban youth construct a practice of science in their lives in ways that are enriching, empowering, and transformative? In what ways does their practice of science intersect with the issues that frame their lives?
- How might the science-teaching practice we construct with youth in urban poverty reflect their lives, their concerns, and their practices of science?

LOOKING ACROSS THE THEMES THAT FRAME YOUTH'S PRACTICES OF SCIENCE

In answering these questions, we have examined the importance, scope, and focus of youth's practices of science. We have used the phrase *a practice of science* to describe what youth *do* with and in science—how they understand, use, and produce science in the different domains that make up their lives. We have traced their participation in science events and the kinds of structures, identities, and relationships they draw on and activate for that participation. Our analysis has revealed the importance of four main themes characterizing youth's practices of science (see Figure 8.1):

- Power and co-opting science spaces
- Relevant science and activating resources
- Transformations: Science as a tool for change
- Community

Each of these themes highlights a desire to be listened to and valued; a deeply personal belief in equity and justice; a longing to matter and a desire to bring about change; and a knowledge that even though students' knowledge, skills, and other forms of expertise are not always valued in school, youth can and should be valued in their own spaces for doing science.

The first crosscutting theme, *power and co-opting science spaces*, highlighted the youth's abilities to understand, participate in, and sometimes change the boundaries of a science event. It showed how youth disrupted the structures that support a science event and the identities and relationships they brought to bear on that process when the science event reduced their authority or power.

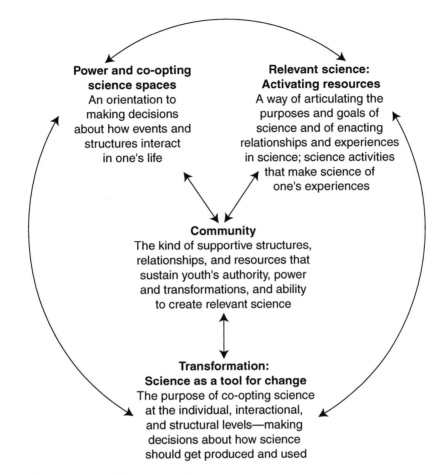

Figure 8.1. Youth's practice of science.

The second crosscutting theme, *relevant science and activating resources*, presented youth's practices of science as a way of articulating the purposes and goals of science and of enacting science activities that make science of one's experiences rather than merely linking science to that experience. It showed how youth used the material, human, and social resources to which they had access in nonstandard ways in order to participate in science and in order to work toward goals that mattered.

The third crosscutting theme, *transformation: science as a tool for change*, presented youth's practices of science as the purpose for using one's space in the borderland to make decisions about how science should get produced, used, and experienced in relationships.

The fourth crosscutting theme, *community*, reflected the kind of supportive structures, relationships, and resources that sustain youth's authority, power and transformations, and abilities to create relevant science.

Thus, these themes show how a practice of science is meant to communicate the importance of focusing not only on what youth learn and how they learn it but also on *how* and *why* urban youth engage in science in the different domains of their lives and how that engagement changes across these different domains.

Youth's practice of science as traced through these four themes moves us from thinking about the goals of science education as being only about the acquisition of a set of concepts and skills to how and why youth activate these concepts and skills with a particular goal or objective in mind. Practices therefore involve actions, but they also draw out how those actions are deeply rooted in ideologies, contexts, cultures, and relationships.

QUESTIONING THE FUTURE

If we apply our understandings of youth's practices of science to our efforts in urban science education, then we may be able to develop a more comprehensive framework for working with students, their families, and community members and school officials who work and live in high-poverty, urban centers. However, we also believe that much more work needs to be done if we are to really transform science education for urban youth in poverty.

We therefore conclude this text by raising one final question: *What kinds of science events, structures, and relationships help students to view science as a transformative influence in their lives and communities?*

In looking across these themes, we can make certain claims about the role and importance of using events, structures, and identities and relationships to make sense of youth's practices of science. In particular, we see three underlying goals that frame youth's efforts to co-opt science spaces, create relevant science, enact agency, and build sustaining communities:

- Thinking about events through multiple points of entry
- Thinking about structures through recognizing networks
- Thinking about identities and relationships through a desire for change

Each of these goals both extends our thinking around youth's practices of science and how those practices are framed through science events, science structures such as space and capital, and identities and relationships. Although each goal is connected to events, structures or identities, and relationships, these constructs and how they played out in the youth's lives are intertwined. So in our discussion of each point, we highlight the importance of each construct but do so in relation to the others.

Thinking About Events: Points of Entry

Co-opting science spaces and activating resources in nonstandard ways all within a supportive community allowed the students to have different points of entry to doing science, not all of which were science oriented or even academic. Specifically, engaging in a practice of science involved many different values, experiences, practices, and people, all of which went into making science a viable place for the children to transform their lives and the science they do. For instance, entry into the picnic table process for Junior was through a strong desire to create a place to play that he and the other children could call their own. There were many stages involved in the picnic table project, including initial sketches, estimating sizes and angles, making accurate blueprints, building small-scale models, preparing a work plan, actually building and troubleshooting the building process, and so on. There were some points at which Junior, like Juan, struggled with the cognitive aspects of this experience—that work that is traditionally deemed "more scientific." There were many more aspects that were a part of the experience than just the cognitive work, and, because these other aspects were valued, they helped Junior and Juan to struggle through what appeared to be more difficult for them.

Iris often chose to enter or exit a project based on whether her siblings could participate, whether it was real, or whether it helped to challenge others' conceptions of her. Iris became once again involved in the nature trail–building experience, after her initial rejection, when she learned that she could build a five-foot-tall great-tailed grackle (*Quiscalus mexicanus*) home that she eventually painted in the colors of the Mexican flag (see Figure 8.2). Grackles are a very common urban bird in Texas that are often looked on as a nuisance, especially in outdoor eating venues. However, they are a beautiful and remarkable bird that clearly lived in and around Hope Shelter. In part Iris was interested in learning about the great-tailed grackle and how a bird home might be built that would appropriately suit these birds. However, her entry into the experience was more about access and power and exerting her identity than it was about what we might more traditionally label as science.

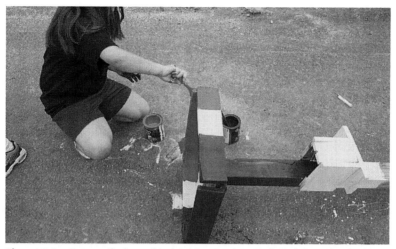

Figure 8.2. Great-tailed grackle bird house (painted as the Mexican flag).

Kobe's entry into the lot project was through his relationships with his peers and their support of his contributions to the video project. Many barriers had to be maneuvered for Kobe's participation in science, with his adversity to academic tasks being only one example. However, this "nonscience" entry point into the lot project influenced Kobe in his wanting to become a scientist.

Other students had more traditional entry points into science activities. Ruben and Darkside, though they both appreciated their roles as leaders and both had desires to use science in ways that would be transformative in their communities, felt comfortable with their academic abilities and often entered projects via their ability to do the scientific work that was demanded.

In the end, however, the practices of science that were created and supported by the youth allowed them to be open to different points of entry into the different science events. As teachers, we could use these entry points to enhance participation. Equally as important, we could also use our understandings of multiple entry points to deepen our understandings of youth's practices of science. For instance, we could use standard measures to determine just how much science Junior, Iris, Juan, Darkside, or any other student learned, and this could be important (e.g., what are grackles' migration patterns? How does the climate of New York City affect what kinds of plants might survive in a community garden?). However, it would only tell part of the story of their science experience and achievement.

Thinking About Structures: Recognizing Networks

Understanding how youth act within power relations and create science practices to transform those power relations provides insight into how the practice of science itself is stretched across people and situations and things. Youth's practices of science exist within relationships between individuals, organizations, and subjects of study. This crosscutting goal builds directly on the previous goal, which indicates that the practice of science among youth is an active and changing process that invites and resists participation in many different ways.

Understanding that practices of science happen within networks means at least two things. First, it means understanding how youth's practices are deeply tied to structures—to the *spaces* where science happens and to the *resources* available for activation there. To better understand how youth's practices of science are tied to structure, we have found it helpful to trace how they have been crafted or stretched across and within those structures. In the lot project (Chapter 6), in order to understand what Darkside's practice of science looked like we had to consider this network in a variety of ways: We had to consider a variety of project components, including the video project, the book, the community meetings and Community Days, and so on. We also had to consider the relationships he established within each one of those projects: with researchers, teachers, other peers, and members of the community. We also had to consider how those relationships were mediated by the resources to which he had access: what he knew about his community, science, architecture, and activism. Finally, we also had to consider how his actions and beliefs influenced the other students, teachers, and community members in their own scope and focus of participation.

Second, understanding that practices of science happen within networks means that that we cannot look at youth's involvement in science as a singular endeavor. We have to understand that youth, and any science they do, exist in a much larger network. Further, we have to understand the science that emerges—in both its content and form—as a product of the entire network. For example, we can trace Ruben's participation in the picnic table–building experiences, but unless we also trace Ruben's relationships to other individuals and other structures, we miss out on the complete story of what he did or learned.

Likewise, we cannot see the science as only being in the activity, such as the design and building of the picnic table itself. We have to understand how different students entered into and exited the project for different reasons and how those different reasons shaped what was done, when, and why. The science was just as much emergent from Junior and his brother

Ruben's attempt to build a place for kids to play as it was in Iris's desire to teach her younger brother how to use the electric drill. In the lot transformation project, the science was just as much as about documenting, cleaning, and renovating a lot as it was about communicating a message to the larger community about what youth can do and about the importance of neighborhood.

Thinking About Identities and Relationships Through a Desire for Change

Cutting across each of our four themes is a desire on the part of the youth for change—whether that change be in their relationships with and in science, in how science is taught to them or applied in their lives, or in the kinds of resources they can and should be allowed to activate to do science. Darkside's story showed us how many of the youth created practices of science that changed the neighborhood and perceptions of the neighborhood. Iris's and Junior's stories show us how youth created science practices that allowed them to change how power was enacted in relationships. Ruben's story (and the shortened stories of the involvement of the other children in the picnic table project) illustrate the power of the youth's practices of science in locating and activating human, social, and material resources in ways that were nontraditional, and in ways that ultimately transform what science was done, how it was done, and how it was viewed by the teachers. Claudia's and Juan's stories show us how youth create practice of science that refuse to acknowledge margin and center dichotomies.

For the youth in our studies, a desire for change is rooted in three principal ideas: change is radical, political, and grounded in their own lives and in their communities.

The youth in our study engaged in science practices that transformed in far-reaching and admirable ways how or why science was taught to them. They challenged who teachers expected them to be or act. They challenged what resources were useful and when. They challenged the very meaning of science and its role in schools or after-school programs by the ways in which they appropriated or resisted science activities.

The youth in our study also engaged in a practice of science that was political—that was meant to influence. They intended to transform relationships—between teachers and students and between individuals and communities and science and society—and transform how we view the relationship between epistemology and ontology. The youth showed us how doing science and learning science is always about relationships,

passionately. Standing at the corner of the garden waving his hands in the air for emphasis). I put a little effort into it. We are going to have to change this garden to make it the best. We have to get a group of people to help us. Our group will do it. We will make a difference, make it better than before. We will make it into a beautiful community. A better community. A better environment, like it was before. (Darkside narrating the last scene of *The Urban Atmosphere*)

Data on Target Children

Number of children followed, 1995–2001:

    35

Number of years over which data were collected for target children:

Less than 1 year	4 children
1 year	20 children
2 years	11 children

Race/Ethnicity:

16 African American children
16 Latino/a children
3 White children

Gender:

20 boys, 15 girls

Participation in Science Program:

30 children who participated in the program
5 children who either did not participate at all or participated only
    minimally

Approximate data generated for each child:

2.5 hours of individual interviews
2 hours of group interviews (two sessions)
10 hours of participant observation notes per child
1-hour interview with mother
1-hour interview with school science teacher
2 hours of (collective) interviews with after-school programs
    coordinator/social worker at shelter
Collection of school science work (products, grades)
Collection of after-school science work (products, authentic
    assessment products, photos, video) (except two children who
    had minimal participation in the SP)
Several hours of informal conversation through participation in
    after-school program (except two children who had minimal
    participation in the SP)
Basic demographic data sheet

Child Study Framework

I. Factual Information
  A. Demographic
    1. Age
    2. Gender
    3. Ethnicity
  B. Incoming Resources
    1. Parental Education/Literacy/Socioeconomic Status
    2. Native Language; Other Language(s); Dominant Language; Language(s) used at home, at school
    3. Immigrant Generation—e.g., country of child's birth, country of mother's birth
    4. Immigrant Legal Status
    5. Access to resources (home computers, books, materials, etc.)
  C. Host-Culture Variables
    1. Time in the U.S.? in [your city]? at [your shelter]?
  D. Family Cohesion
    1. Family members living at [the shelter], in the U.S., in other countries
    2. Intergenerational and extended-family relationships
  E. Peer Orientation
    1. Who are the student's friends? How do they associate, when, and why?
    2. Who does the child have particular problems with (if at all and why)?
  F. General School/Extracurricular Experiences
    1. School attended
    2. What kind of program is the student in? Bilingual?
    3. Time attending that school, program

Aspects of this framework adapted from Suárez-Orozco & Suárez-Orozco, 1999.

4. Grade
5. Teacher(s)
6. Achievement: grades, report cards
7. Involvement in other after-school programs (which? why? where?)
8. Involvement in extracurricular activities (which? why? where?)
9. Parental role in schooling
10. Demographics of classmates, teachers
11. Past school experiences and lengths of time at different schools, in different programs (bilingual?)
12. Has the student ever been to school in another country?
  G. Science/Technology Experiences (in and out of school)
1. How often do students receive science instruction in school?
2. How does science compare to other subjects in time, emphasis?
3. How often do students have access to computers in school? Out of school?
4. What kind of computers are available? Where?
5. What kind of computing do the students engage in? When and where?
II. Attitudes, Perceptions, Beliefs (APB)
  A. About Self
1. Perceptions of racism, classism, and sexism
2. Long-term goals
3. Current challenges, obstacles
4. Special interests, needs
5. Past experiences of importance
6. Agency: do they see themselves as being able to make changes in their own lives or their community?
7. Power: APB about their position in power relationships (in family, in school, at [the shelter])
8. Voice
  B. About Family
1. Positive/negative experiences with family
2. APB about their role in their family
  C. About Friends
1. Positive/negative experiences with friends
2. Positive/negative experiences with nonfriend peers
3. Why/how do they select their friends?
4. How does living at [the shelter] affect friendships (at school, at [the shelter], or between school and [the shelter])?
  D. About Community (especially [the shelter])
1. Positive/negative experiences with [the shelter] and/or [the shelter] staff

2. To what degree is [the shelter] identified as their "community"?
3. What aspects do they see as being part of their community? How?
4. What communities would they identify as more meaningful to them?
5. What is the impact of the larger nonneighborhood surrounding [the shelter]?
6. What are their APB about their role in community?
7. Does the student feel separated from "outside U.S. culture"?
8. Agency: Do they see themselves as being able to make changes in their community?
9. Power: APB about the power structures/relationships at [the shelter]
10. Fear of violence?
11. Ideas about future community

E. About School and Teachers
1. Positive/negative experiences with school
2. Favorite/least favorite school subject(s) and why
3. Best/worst school subject(s) and why
4. Favorite/least favorite teacher(s) and why
5. What is their relationship with their favorite/least favorite teachers? How do the students imagine these teachers are perceiving them?
6. APB about succeeding in school
7. Are their personal experiences (including language, race, identity), home life, community life reflected in school (curriculum and/or pedagogy)?
8. How do they gauge the usefulness of their school experiences?
9. What do they see as the purposes of schooling? What is it for? What *should* it be for?
10. What would they change about school or their teachers?
11. What does it mean to be "intelligent" or "smart"?

F. About the After-School Program (ASP)
1. Positive/negative experience with the ASP and/or ASP volunteers
2. Are your personal experiences, home life, community life reflected in the ASP?
3. APB about impact of ASP activities on community, [the shelter], their families, their lives
4. How do they gauge the usefulness of their ASP experiences?
5. What do they see as the purposes of ASP? What is/should it be for?

     6. What would they change about the ASP?

     7. Also: questions and conversations about ASP projects (picnic table, nature trail, etc.)

G. About Science

     1. Positive/negative experiences with science in school

     2. Positive/negative experiences with science in after-school science

     3. Why would they or could they do science out of school?

     4. What is science?

     5. Why study science

     6. APB about succeeding science, math, and technology

     7. Role of science in society, in local community, at [the shelter], in their families

     8. Do their friends like science? Use science? Do science?

     9. Does their family like science? Use science? Do science?

    10. What would they change about "science" or the way science is taught?

Notes

CHAPTER 1

1. All children's names are pseudonyms, selected by the children themselves, used in order to protect their identities. Additionally, all names of schools, community organizations, and localities (with the exception of New York City) are pseudonyms.

2. None of these poverty statistics include families living in homeless shelters because, according to the Census Bureau, it is too difficult for census workers to keep track of transient families.

3. Forty-six percent of African American children and 40% of Hispanic children live below the poverty line, compared with 16% of White children.

4. Not all the stories about children in urban poverty or urban children experiencing homelessness are quantitative—simply the majority. Two excellent qualitative stories are Polakow, 1993, and Quint, 1994.

5. We use the word *homed* to refer to nonhomeless persons.

6. These policies include such things as slashed public assistance, reduced food stamps, cuts in housing assistance, denied Earned Income Tax Credits, and cuts in welfare spending.

7. Since the figure cited here is for K–12 (approximately ages 5–18), it does not account for pre-K or preschool, or birth through age 4.

CHAPTER 2

1. There are notable exceptions, which are raised later in this section. In particular, see the articles published in the "Urban Science Education" issues of *JRST* (2001, *JRST, 38* (8–10)).

2. For a more complete discussion of the deficit model and the current reform initiatives in science education, see Calabrese Barton and Osborne (2001).

CHAPTER 7

1. For a more detailed discussion of this project, involving the abandoned lot, see Fusco, 2001. For a discussion of what youth learned and how their progress was assessed, see Fusco and Calabrese Barton, 2001.

2. Although these steps appear linear and preset, they are only a useful heuristic (applied after the fact) for describing the events that made up the project.

References

Aikenhead, G. (1997). Towards a First Nations cross-cultural science and technology curriculum. *Science Education, 81*, 217–238.

American Association for the Advancement of Science. (1989). *Science for all Americans: Project 2061*. Washington, DC: American Association for the Advancement of Science Press.

American Association for the Advancement of Science. (1993). *Benchmarks for scientific literacy*. New York: Oxford University Press.

Anyon, J. (1997). *Ghetto schooling*. New York: Teachers College Press.

Anzaldúa, G. (1987). *Borderlands, la frontera: The new mestiza*. San Francisco: Aunt Lute Books.

Ayers, W. (1996). *City kids, city teachers: Reports from the front row*. New York: New Press.

Barton, D., Hamilton, M., & Ivanic, R. (2000). *Situated literacies: Reading and writing in context*. New York: Routledge.

Battistich, V., Solomon, D., Kim, D., Watson, K., & Schaps, E. (1995). Schools as communities, poverty levels of student populations, and students' attitudes, motives, and performance: A multilevel analysis. *American Education Research Journal, 32*(3), 627–658.

Beard, R. (1987). *On being homeless: Historical perspectives*. New York: Museum of the City of New York.

Bernal, D. D. (1998). Using a Chicana feminist epistemology in educational research. *Harvard Educational Review, 68*(4), 555–582.

Bouillion, L., & Gomez, L. (2001). Connecting school and community with science learning: Real world problems and school-community partnerships as contextual scaffolds. *Journal of Research in Science Teaching, 38*(8), 878–899.

Bourdieu, P. (1977). *Outline of a theory of practice* (Richard Nice, Trans.). Cambridge, England: Cambridge University Press.

Brickhouse, N. (1994). Bringing in the outsiders: Reshaping the sciences of the future. *Journal of Curriculum Studies, 26*(4), 401–428.

Brickhouse, N., & Potter, J. (2001). Young women's scientific identity formation in an urban context. *Journal of Research in Science Teaching, 38*(8), 965–980.

Calabrese Barton, A. (1998). Science education and the politics of poverty. *Educational Policy, 12*(5), 525–541.

Calabrese Barton, A. (2001). Capitalism, critical pedagogy, and urban science education: A conversation with Peter McLaren. *Journal of Research in Science Teaching, 38*(8), 847–860.

Calabrese Barton, A., & Darkside (2000). Autobiography in science education: Greater objectivity through local knowledge. *Research in Science Education, 30*(1), 23–42.

Calabrese Barton, A., & Osborne, M. D. (Eds.) (2001). *Teaching science in diverse settings: Marginalized discourses and classroom practice.* New York: Peter Lang.

Calabrese Barton, A., & Yang, K. (2000). The culture of power and science education: Learning from Miguel. *Journal of Research in Science Teaching, 37*(8), 871–889.

Casey, K. (1993). *I Answer with my life: Life histories of women teachers working for social change.* New York: Routledge.

Clandinin, D. J., & Connelly, F. M. (2000). *Narrative inquiry: Experience and story in qualitative research.* San Francisco: Jossey-Bass.

Cobern, W. W. (1996). Worldview theory and conceptual change in science education. *Science Education, 80*(5), 579–610.

Costa, V. B. (1995). When science is "another world": Relationships between worlds of family, friends, school, and science. *Science Education, 79*(3), 313–333.

Council of the Great City Schools. (1994). *National urban education goals: 1992–1993 indicator report.* Washington, DC: Author.

Council of the Great City Schools. (2001). Beating the odds II. *A city-by-city analysis of student performance and achievement gaps on state assessments.* http://www.cgcs.org/taskforce/ reports/beat_the_oddsII.html. August 2001.

Dalaker, J. (2001). *Poverty in the United States: 2000.* Washington, DC: U.S. Census Bureau.

Darling-Hammond, L. (1999). America's future: Educating teachers. *The Education Digest, 64*(9), 18–35.

Delgado-Gaitan, C. (1996). *Protean literacy: Extending the discourse on empowerment.* London: Falmer Press.

Delgado-Gaitan, C., & Trueba, H. (1991). *Crossing cultural borders: Education for immigrant families in American.* New York: Falmer Press.

de Nunez, R. (1995). Family values among homeless families. *Journal of the American Public Welfare Association, 53.*

Duschl, R. (1990). *Restructuring science education: The importance of theories and their development.* New York: Teachers College Press.

Education Trust. (1996). *Education watch: The 1998 education trust state and national data book.* Washington, DC: Author.

Eisenhart, M., & Finkel, E. (1999). *Women's science: Learning and succeeding from the margins.* Chicago: University of Chicago Press.

Eisenhart, M., Finkel, E., & Marion, S. (1996). Creating the conditions for scientific literacy: A re-examination. *American Education Research Journal, 33*(2), 261–295.

Elenes, A. (2001). Transformando fronteras: Chicana feminist transformative pedagogies. *International Journal of Qualitative Studies in Education, 14*(5), 689–702.

Farrell, E. (1991). *Hanging in and dropping out.* New York: Teachers College Press.

Fine, M. (1991). *Framing dropouts: Notes on the politics of an urban high school.* New York: State University of New York Press.

Fordham, S. (1996). *Blacked out: Dilemmas of race, identity, and success at Capital High.* Chicago: University of Chicago Press.

Freire, P. (1971). *Pedagogy of the oppressed.* New York: Continuum.

Freire, P. (1993). *Pedagogy of the city.* New York: Continuum.

Freire, P. (1996). *Letters to Cristina: Reflections on my life and work.* New York: Routledge.

Freire, P. (1997). *Pedagogy of the heart.* New York: Continuum.

Freire, P. (1998). *Pedagogy of freedom: Ethics, democracy, and civic courage.* Lanham, MD: Rowman & Littlefield.

Fusco, D. (2001). Creating relevant science through urban planning and gardening. *Journal of Research in Science Teaching, 38*(8), 860–888.

Fusco, D., & Calabrese Barton, A. (2001). Re-presenting student achievement in science. *Journal of Research in Science Teaching, 38*(3), 337–354.

Gilbert, A., & Yerrick, R. (2001). Same school, separate worlds: A sociocultural study of identity, resistance, and negotiated in a rural, lower track science classroom, *Journal of Research in Science Teaching, 38*(5), 574–598.

Goodson, I. (1992). *Studying teachers' lives.* London: Routledge.

Gourlay, K. (1992). *World of waste: Dilemmas of industrial development.* Atlantic Heights, NJ: Zed Books.

Hamilton, M. (2000). Expanding new literacy studies: Using photographs to explore literacy as social practice. In D. Barton, M. Hamilton, & R. Ivanic (Eds.), *Situated literacies: Reading and writing in context* (pp. 16–34). New York: Routledge.

Hammond, L. (2001). Notes from California: An anthropological approach to urban science education for language minority families. *Journal of Research in Science Teaching, 38*(9), 983–1000.

Harding, S. (1998). *Is science multicultural? Postcolonialisms, feminisms, and epistemologies.* Bloomington: Indiana University Press.

Heath, S. B. (1982). Protean shapes in literacy events: Ever shifting oral and literate traditions. In D. Tannen (Ed.), *Spoken and written language: Exploring orality and literacy* (pp. 91–117). Norwood, NJ: Ablex.

Heath, S. B. (1999). Rethinking youth transitions. *Human Development, 42*(6), 376–382.

Hill, G., Atwater, M., & Wiggins, J. (1995). Attitudes toward science of urban seventh-grade life science students over time, and the relationship to future plans, family, teacher, curriculum, and school. *Urban Education, 30*(1), 71–92.

Hodson, D. (1999). Going beyond cultural pluralism: Science education for sociopolitical action. *Science Education, 83*, 775–796.

Homes for the Homeless. (2001). *Déjà vu: Family homelessness in New York City: A report of the Institute for Children and Poverty.* New York: Institute for Children and Poverty.

hooks, b. (1984). *Feminist theory: From margin to center.* Boston: South End Press.

Hutchinson, J. N. (1999). *Students on the margins.* Albany: State University of New York Press.

Ingersoll, R. (1999). The problem of underqualified teachers in American secondary schools. *Educational Researcher, 28*(2), 26–30.

Keller, E. (1985). *Reflections on gender and science.* New Haven: Yale University Press.

Krajcik, J., Czerniak, C., & Berger, C. (1999). *Teaching children science: A project-based approach.* New York: McGraw-Hill.

Kuhn, T. S. (1962). *The structure of scientific revolutions.* Chicago: University of Chicago Press.

Kyle, W. (1999). Science education in developing countries: Access, equity, and ethical responsibility. *Journal of the Southern African Association for Research in Mathematics and Science Education, 3*(1), 1–13.

Kyle, W. (2001). Toward a political philosophy of science education. In Calabrese Barton & M. Osborne (Eds.), *Teaching science in diverse settings* (pp. xi–xix). New York: Peter Lang.

Latour, B. (1987). *Science in action.* Cambridge, MA: Harvard University Press.

Latour, B. (1993). *We have never been modern.* Cambridge, MA: Harvard University Press.

Lave, J. (1988). *Cognition in practice: Mind, mathematics, and culture in everyday life.* Cambridge, UK: Cambridge University Press.

Lave, J., & Wenger, E. (1991). *Situated learning: Legitimate peripheral participation.* Cambridge, UK: Cambridge University Press.

Lee, O., & Fradd, S. H. (1998). Science for all, including students from non-English-language backgrounds. *Educational Researcher, 27,* 12–21.

McAdams, D. P. (1993). *The stories we live by: Personal myths and the making of self.* New York: Guilford Press.

McGinn, M. K., & Roth, W.-M. (1999). Preparing students for competent scientific practice: Implications of recent research in science and technology studies. *Educational Researcher, 28,* 14–24.

McLaren, P. (1989). *Life in schools: An introduction to critical pedagogy in the foundations of education.* New York: Longman.

McLaren, P. (1992). Collisions with otherness: traveling theory, post-colonial criticism, and the politics of ethnographic practice—the mission of the wounded ethnographer. *Qualitative Studies in Education, 5*(1), 77–92.

McLaughlin, M., Irby, M., & Langman, J. (1994). *Urban sanctuaries: Neighborhood organizations in the lives and futures of inner-city youth.* San Francisco: Jossey-Bass.

Middlebrooks, S. (1998). *Getting to know city kids.* New York: Teachers College Press.

National Center for Education Statistics. (2002). District characteristics for peer groups. Washington, DC: U.S. Department of Education [Online] Available: http://nces.ed.gov/edfin/search/show_peers.asp?Group=agn&AG_AGID=2201170&parsedQuery=GCS+=+1 (August 1, 2002).

National Center for Health Statistics. (1995). *Current estimates from the National Health Interview Survey, 1994.* Washington, DC: U.S. Dept. of Health and Human Services.

National Law Center on Homelessness and Poverty. (2000). *Separate and unequal: A report on educational barriers for homeless children and youth.* Washington, DC: Author.

National Research Council. (1996). *National Science Education Standards.* Washington, DC: National Academy Press.

National Science Teachers Association. (1996). *NSTA Pathways to the Science Standard.* Washington, DC: Author.

National Science Teachers Association. (1998). *Pathways to National Standards.* Washington, DC: Author.

Nieto, S. (1999). *The light in their eyes: Creating multicultural learning communities.* New York: Teachers College Press.

Oakes, J. (1990). *Multiplying inequalities: The effects of race, social class, and tracking on opportunities to learn mathematics and science.* Santa Monica, CA: RAND.

Oakes, J., Gamoran, A., & Page, R. (1992). Curriculum differentiation: Opportunities, outcomes and meanings. *The Curriculum Handbook* (pp. 570–608). New York: Macmillan.

Oakes, J., Muir, K., & Joseph, R. (2000). *Coursetaking and achievement: Inequalities that endure and change.* A keynote presentation at the National Institute for Science Education Annual Meeting, Detroit, MI.

Odegaard, M., & Kyle, W. (2000). Imagination and critical reflection: Cultivating a vision of scientific literacy. Submitted to the *Journal of Research in Science Teaching.*

Omerod, F., & Ivanic, R. (2000). Texts in practices: Interpreting the physical characteristics of children's project work. In D. Barton, M. Hamilton, & R. Ivanic (Eds.), *Situated literacies: Reading and writing in context* (pp. 91–107). New York: Routledge.

Osborne, M. D. (1998). Responsive science pedagogy in a democracy: Dangerous teaching. *Theory Into Practice, 37*(4), 225–237.

Page, R. (1989). The lower-track curriculum at a "heavenly" high school: "Cycles of prejudice." *Journal of Curriculum Studies, 21*(3), 197–208.

Page, R. (1990). Games of chance: The lower-track curriculum in a college-preparatory high school. *Curriculum Inquiry, 20*(3), 249–264.

Payne, R. (1998). *A framework for understanding poverty.* Highlands, TX: RFT.

Personal Narratives Group. (1989). *Interpreting women's lives: Feminist theory and personal narratives.* Bloomington, IN: Indiana University Press.

Polakow, V. (1993). *Lives on the edge.* Chicago: University of Chicago Press.

Quint, S. (1994). *Schooling homeless children: A working model for America's public schools.* New York: Teachers College Press.

Rahm, J. (2002). Emergent learning opportunities in an inner city gardening program. *Journal of Research in Science Teaching, 39*(2), 164–184.

Rodriguez, A. (1997). The dangerous discourse of invisibility. *Journal of Research in Science Teaching, 34*(1), 19–38.

Rodriguez, A. (1998). Strategies for counterresistance: Toward sociotransformative constructivism and learning to teach science for diversity and for understanding. *Journal of Research in Science Teaching, 35*(6), 589–608.

Rodriguez, A. (2001). From gap gazing to promising cases: Moving toward equity in urban education reform. *Journal of Research in Science Teaching, 38*(10), 1115–1130.

Roth, W. M., & McGinn, M. (1999). Preparing students for competent scientific practice: Implications of recent research in science and technology studies. *Educational Researcher, 28*(3), 14–24.

Roth, W. M., Tobin, K., Elmesky, R., Carambo, C., McKight, Y., & Beers, J. (in press). Re/making identities in the praxis of urban schooling: A cultural historical perspective. *Mind, Culture, & Activity.*

Science Research Council of Canada. (1984). *Science for every citizen: Educating Canadians for tomorrow's world, Summary of Report No. 36.* Ottawa: Supply and Service.

Seiler, G. (2001). Reversing the standard direction: Science emerging from the lives of African-American students. *Journal of Research in Science Teaching, 38*(9), 1000–1115.

Seiler, G., Tobin, K., & Sokolic, J. (2001). Roadblocks on the path to understanding technology and science. *Journal of Research in Science Teaching, 38,* 746–767.

Seiler, G., Tobin, K., & Sokolic, J. (2003). Reconstituting resistance in urban science education. *Journal of Research in Science Teaching, 40,* 101–103.

Sewell, W. H. (1992). A theory of structure: Duality, agency, and transformation. *American Journal of Sociology, 98,* 1–29.

Spillane, J. P., Diamond, J., Walker, L., Havelson, R., & Jita, L. (2001). Urban school leadership for elementary science instruction: Identifying and activating resources in an undervalued school subject. *Journal of Research in Science Teaching, 38*(8), 918–941.

Stanley, W., & Brickhouse, N. (1995). Multiculturalism, universalism, and science education. *Science Education, 78*(4), 387–398.

Stanley, W., & Brickhouse, N. (2001). Teaching sciences: The multicultural question revisited. *Science Education, 85*(1), 35–50.

Street, B. (1998). Literacies in theory and practice: What are the implications for language in education? *Linguistics in Education, 10*(1), 1–24.

Suárez-Orozco, M., & Suárez-Orozco, M. (1999). A conceptual framework for understanding immigrant youth. In H. Trueba & L. Bartalome (Eds.), *Immigrant voices: In search of educational equity* (pp. 37–74). Lanham, MD: Rowman & Littlefield.

Swidler, A. (1986). Culture in action: Symbols and strategies. *American Sociological Review, 51,* 273–286.

Tobin, K., Roth, W. M., & Zimmerman, A. (2001). 16. Learning to teach science in urban schools. *Journal of Research in Science Teaching, 38*(8), 941–965.

Tobin, K., Seiler, G., & Walls, E. (1999). Reproduction of social class in the teaching and learning of science in urban high schools. *Research in Science Education, 29,* 171–187.

U.S. Census Bureau. (2001). *National demographic profile.* Washington, DC: U.S. Census Bureau Public Information Office.

U.S. Department of Education. National Center for Education Statistics. (1996). *Urban schools: The challenge and location of poverty.* Washington, DC: Author.

Valenzuela, A. (1999). *Subtractive schooling: U.S.-Mexican youth and the politics of caring.* Albany: State University of New York Press.

Vygotsky, L. S. (1978). *Mind in society: The development of higher psychological processes.* Cambridge, MA: Harvard University Press.

Ward, J. (2000). Raising resisters: The role of truth telling in the psychological development of African-American girls. In L. Weis & M. Fine (Eds.), *Construction sites: Excavating race, class, and gender among urban youth*. New York: Teachers College Press.

Weinstein, M. (2002, April). *Reversing the objective: Adding guinea pig pedagogies*. A paper presented at the National Association for Research in Science Teaching, New Orleans, LA.

Wilkinson, J. (1847). *Science for all: A lecture*. London: William Newberg.

Witherell, C., & Noddings, N. (1991). *Stories lives tell: Narrative and dialog in education*. New York: Teachers College Press.

Index

Italicized page numbers refer to figures and tables.

Suburbs, 7, 151–53
Swidler, A., 39
Symbolic resources, 39, 48, 49

Tanahia: and living in borderland, 46–47,
56, 57–58, 59–60; and power and co-
opting science spaces, 73–74, 75, 76; and
relevant science, 100, 101, 102, 108
Tanda, 91, 121, 142–44, 145, 146–47, 148,
149, 150
Teachers: adversarial relationship between
student and, 20, 23, 24; and building
communities, 138, 153, 156; certification
of, 24; and change, 122, 124–25, 126, 127,
131, 135; and co-opting science spaces,
68–69, 70, 77, 79–80, 86; and critical
approach, 28; and empowering science
education, 158, 159, 165, 166, 167; and
living in borderland, 46, 47, 48, 53–54,
55, 57–58, 59, 62; as mean, 46, 48, 53–54,
57–58, 102, 159; power of, 24, 68–69, 70,
77, 79–80, 86; and practice of science, 35,
138, 153, 156, 158, 159, 165, 166, 167;
and relevant science, 100, 102, 107–08,
118, 119; and science for all, 23, 24–25,
30; sensitivity-to-poverty training for,
62; and stories as making case for urban
science education, 7. *See also specific
student*
Tests, standardized, 7, 12, 24, 53, 76, 77
Texas Assessment of Academic Skills
(TAAS), 76, 77, 80, 81
Texas Essential Knowledge and Skills
(TEKS), 111, *112*
Tobin, K., 32, 33, 41, 68, 69, 70–71
Top Hill. *See* Southside Shelter
Tornado activity, 88
Tracking, 24–25
Transformation. *See* Change
Tunnel-building project, 1–4, 9, 16, 64, 83–
84

UNESCO, 25
The Urban Atmosphere (video): and building
communities, 142–43, 145–46, 147, 151,
156; and change, 120–21, 130, 131; and
contradictions between in-school and
out-of-school science, 23; and science for
all, 30, 32; and social justice, 168–69

Urban settings: practice of science in, 34–
43; and science for all, 23–33; statistics
about poverty in, 6–7; suburbs
compared with, 7, 151–53. *See also
specific topic*
U.S. Census Bureau, 6
U.S. Department of Education, 6

Valenzuela, A., 31
Video: and building communities, 142–
43, 145–46, 147, 151, 156; of Claudia,
54; of Darkside, 91, 120–21, 130, 131,
165, 168–69; and empowering science,
164, 165, 168–69; of Kobe, 23, 30, 32,
164
Voting, 66, 67
Vygotsky, L., 28

Walker, L., 32, 39
Walls, E., 33, 41, 68, 69, 70
Ward, J., 50
Water balloon experiment, 61
Watson, K., 153
Weather activity, 77, 80
Weinstein, M., 38
Well Springs, Texas. *See* Hope Shelter
Wenger, E., 28, 39
What science, question about, 155–56
Where question, 154–55
Wiggins, J., 25
Wilkinson, J., 25
Witherell, C., 7, 8
Women: and science for all, 26–27, 30–31.
See also Feminism
Worldviews, 9, 40–41, 116, 167
Writing reports, 54

Yang, K., 69
Yerrick, R., 68, 69, 70
Yolanda, 146
Youth: assumptions about, 27; and
building communities, 138–57;
challenges facing, 138; and community,
153–56; concerns of, 5, 18, 139; lack of
trust of knowledge of, 107–08, 117; and
science education, 153–56;
transformation of worlds of, 120

Zimmermann, A., 32

About the Authors

Angela Calabrese Barton is an associate professor of science education at Teachers College, Columbia University. She has been teaching and researching with homeless youth for seven years. Before that, she was a chemistry teacher at a community college and a chemist. She is the author of *Feminist Science Education*, and her research has been published in the *Journal of Research in Science Teaching*, *Curriculum Inquiry*, the *Journal of Teacher Education*, and *Qualitative Studies in Education*, among other scholarly journals.

A native of Pittsburgh, Jason Ermer took his undergraduate degree in computer science and spent two years working in the high-tech industry before earning a master's degree in education from the University of Texas at Austin. He is currently a mathematics and computer science educator in the Kealing Junior High School Magnet Program in Austin, Texas.

Tanahia Burkett is an elementary school teacher in the New Orleans Parish public schools. She completed her master's degree in curriculum and instruction at the University of Texas at Austin in 2000.

Margery Osborne is an associate professor of science education at the University of Illinois at Urbana-Champaign. She is the author of *Constructing and Framing Knowledge in the Elementary School Classroom: Teachers, Students, and Science*, and has published her research in a number of journals, including the *Journal of Research in Science Teaching*, the *Journal of Curriculum Studies*, and *Qualitative Studies in Education*.